T0365819

Blessed Virgin Mary, Mother of All Nations, Pray for Us

By: Patricia J. Vázquez

GOD'S LOVE, MIRACLES, MESSAGES, AND PRAYERS

WestBow Press books may be ordered through booksellers or by contacting:

WestBow Press
A Division of Thomas Nelson & Zondervan
1663 Liberty Drive
Bloomington, IN 47403
www.westbowpress.com
1 (866) 928-1240

ISBN: 978-1-4908-2772-8 (sc)
ISBN: 978-1-4908-2773-5 (e)

Library of Congress Control Number: 2014903674

Printed in the United States of America.

WestBow Press rev. date: 04/04/2014

WESTBOW°
PRESS
A DIVISION OF THOMAS NELSON
& ZONDERVAN

ABOUT PATRICIA VÁZQUEZ

Patricia (hereafter known as Patricia, or she) is a devout Roman Catholic. Patricia grew up in a small rural town, was the third of five children, and attended Catholic grade school. She went on to public high school, and then to college, getting her Bachelor of Arts with a major in Industrial Relations, and a minor in Business Administration. She is married and she and her husband have two children. Patricia worked for fourteen years and then resigned to stay home and raise her children; she also did volunteer work. Patricia enjoys baking, crocheting, and various crafts. Patricia and her husband feel blessed with many graces to have had their home enthroned by a Catholic Priest to the Sacred Heart of Jesus, according to "St. Louis de Montfort's" prayers for this special home enthronement. At that time, their children were around the ages of four and six years old. This Priest blessed every room in their home with holy water, and then blessed their Sacred Heart of Jesus picture with holy water. Patricia has this beautiful picture hanging on their living room wall.

DEDICATION

TO GOD ALMIGHTY, JESUS CHRIST, OUR SAVIOR, AND HIS SACRED HEART, THE HOLY SPIRIT, THE BLESSED VIRGIN MARY, ST. JOSEPH, TO ST. PADRE PIO OF PIETRELCINA, TO MY HUSBAND AND CHILDREN, MY SISTER LORETTA, TO PRO-LIFE IN ALL ITS STAGES, TO ADOPTION, AND, TO THE YOUTH OF THE WORLD, AS JESUS CHRIST IS DEPICTED AS A YOUNG YOUTH ON THE COVER OF THIS BOOK

APPRECIATION AND THANKSGIVING

Patricia is humbly thankful to God, for seeking her out as his servant, his writer, and to deliver these prayers God wants to be prayed. Dear God, I thank you for the many graces you have sent me through the Holy Spirit to bring these nine days of prayer to fruition and present this manuscript for publishing. Dear God, you said the following, in part: "I accomplish my every purpose." **Isaiah Ch. 46: 10.** Jesus, you said: "Amen, amen, I say to you, you will weep and mourn, while the world rejoices; you will grieve, but your grief will become joy." **John 16: 20.** Patricia is very appreciative of what she feels overall, this gift of love to her in God's INTRODUCTION TO PATRICIA, HOW THE VIRGIN MARY AND HER SON JESUS CHRIST WERE TO APPEAR ON THE COVER OF THIS BOOK, AND THE NINE DAYS OF PRAYER GOD GAVE HER TO WRITE. Dear God, you honor the Blessed Virgin Mary, by giving this title to the book:

"BLESSED VIRGIN MARY, MOTHER OF ALL NATIONS, PRAY FOR US"

TABLE OF CONTENTS

DEFINITION OF THE WORD
"MONSTRANCE" vi

<u>DEFINITION OF THE WORD *"MONSTRANCE"*</u>

A *monstrance* is a receptacle or vessel, usually in the color of gold or silver, for encasing the consecrated Host, which is exposed for adoration. Another name for *monstrance* is *ostensorium.*

AN IMPORTANT PREFACE
AND
PATRICIA'S MIRACLE/SUPERNATURAL EXPERIENCES
**NOTE: READ FIRST EVERYTHING PRIOR TO FIRST DAY OF PRAYER

Patricia wrote this book in two Roman Catholic Church Eucharistic Perpetual Adoration Chapels. Patricia feels strongly that God is calling all of us to seek **holiness in our lives, converting our lives back to God, and God's Ten Commandments. The nine (9) days of prayer are to commemorate a typical nine-month pregnancy.**

Patricia is also very appreciative and thankful to God for showing her, first of all, **the first miracle experience of grace in the Eucharistic Perpetual Adoration Chapel,** and subsequently all the **supernatural/miracle occurrences and images** to persevere in accomplishing this during her journey to bring this book to fruition. Patricia is also in appreciation to a few Roman Catholic Priests that she consulted with; and, also, the priest who gave a prayer and holy water blessing of her picture of Jesus and the Blessed Virgin Mary. Part of the Priest's prayer was: **"That this picture is used for the intentions it is meant to be used."**

Patricia is completing this book based on numerous miracle experiences/ supernatural events for her and the "interior locutions" given by God to her heart. Patricia perceives the locutions aren't really strange, phenomenal, or sensational, but rather a mystical experience, a special gift and grace from God; and, a method God utilizes to communicate with his children. These are not authentic apparitions of God, Jesus, or The Blessed Virgin Mary. Patricia realizes as she receives the messages, that she doesn't hear them in an auditory voice with sound. Patricia prays very often, and has been in devout prayer in her attending daily Mass for many years. Patricia feels in her "messages to her heart," that these are more than a gift from the Holy Spirit, but that she was selected by God because of her strong faith and prayer life. As being the recipient of these messages, and that she perceives these very clear words that are born in her heart; and, when these words are joined together, will be the message and prayers.

Patricia visited a Roman Catholic Church's Eucharistic Perpetual Adoration Chapel with her sister when Patricia was very sick in May, 2008 and they both knelt down on their kneelers to pray. When Patricia and her sister knelt down in the chapel and noticed the outer designed part (about 3 inches in depth) part of the monstrance was silver... Patricia and her sister started praying the holy rosary quietly. While praying the rosary, Patricia's sister quietly said to her: "See the Holy Monstrance now and she did." Patricia and her sister both saw the outer designed part of the monstrance had turned from the silver color to a beautiful blue color, unlike any blue they had seen before; and, never this beautiful blue color on a monstrance. Patricia went to another person in Perpetual Adoration and asked her what color she saw the outer designed part of the Holy Monstrance. She said it was silver. I told her my sister and I see it as this very beautiful blue color. The next day Patricia contacted this Roman Catholic Church's Parish office, and she commented on this beautiful blue color. The office secretary said: "it's not blue, it's silver, the part you're describing; and she asked the Pastor if he saw it as blue, and he said "no, this designed part of the monstrance is silver." The office secretary said: "God must be doing something special for you showing you this part of the Monstrance blue in color," and Patricia agreed. The following week Patricia decided to return to this Perpetual Adoration Chapel to pray, and curious to see if this part of the Monstrance was still this beautiful blue color; it was for her, and she felt in awe once again. Two other adorers were in there at this present time, and Patricia quietly went up to them and asked them what color they saw this outer designed part of the Holy Monstrance; they each said it was silver. Patricia commented to them that she sees it this beautifully colored blue. One of the lady worshipers there said to Patricia: "God must be doing something special for you in showing you this blue color." See further miracles for Patricia listed below this preface section of this book.

MIRACULOUS PICTURE OF BLUE MONSTRANCE IN THE PERPETUAL EUCHARISTIC ADORATION CHAPEL AS PATRICIA SAW IT. PATRICIA ALWAYS THOUGHT WHEN SHE SAW THE BLUE MONSTRANCE THIS BEAUTIFUL COLOR BLUE, THAT THIS REPRESENTED THE BLESSED VIRGIN MARY'S MANTLE AROUND HER SON JESUS.

MIRACLES
SUBSEQUENT MIRACLES (GRACES FROM GOD) HAPPENING FOR PATRICIA

1.

Patricia had a notebook and took it out of her purse and decided she was going to write. God instructed this first time what the title of the book was to be called; and, how His Mother Mary and His Son Jesus were to look in appearance, and the picture in its entirety for the cover of this book. On all subsequent visits to the Eucharistic Perpetual Adoration Chapel, part of the Holy Monstrance was this beautiful blue color, except in her last visit outlined at the end here.

2.

Patricia, during the course of writing this prayer book and **initially** completing it in in the latter part of fall of 2008, (prior to this had taken) much time seeking the spiritual direction of six (6)--all who have seen Patricia's manuscript, Roman Catholic Priests (one saying, **"Jesus is "The Way, The Truth and The Life;"** another Priest saying: **"Follow Jesus."** Another Roman Catholic Priest advised, **"Get this manuscript published."** Then consulting with another Roman Catholic Priest, he also said **"Follow Jesus".** To one of the last two Roman Catholic Priests she last contacted, (who also have a copy of her manuscript) he contacted Patricia and told her that **he really liked "The New Parable of a Mustard Seed" given to her by God her first day of writing at this first Perpetual Adoration Chapel; and he said, in getting your book accomplished, would be doing a great deed for Almighty God.** Patricia is thankful to all the Roman Catholic Priests for taking time to read her manuscript and give her their comments.

3.

During the course of writing this book for the Blessed Trinity, Patricia has been joining a prayer group with a very large white corpus of Jesus on a dark colored large crucifix on the very near left side of this house. To the left of this house and crucifix, is a fenced in clinic that provides abortion services, which are also done on Saturdays, besides other days of the week. Two to four volunteers are there very early in the morning these Saturday's in front of the drive-way to the clinic providing abortion services. They gave out Pro-life literature, with posters of what an aborted baby looks like at various stages of its development; and, then showing them that there is help for them across the street at the Pro-life center,

x

encouraging them not to have an abortion. Every Saturday morning a group of people gather for prayer in front of the large crucifix (next to a fenced in building doing abortions). A Roman Catholic Priest leads the five Glorious, five Sorrowful, and five Joyful Mysteries of the Holy Rosary; and, following with the Prayers of the "Chaplet of Divine Mercy," praying for an end to abortion.

On one occasion in the latter part of May, 2008, following these prayers, a lady in the group asked the Catholic Priest leading the prayers if he noticed Jesus middle toe on one of his feet dripping drops of water during the prayers. The Priest stated "No." Many people had already left, but about eight ladies, including Patricia and her sister, went up to view this dripping middle toe of slow dripping water. He looked at it and didn't quite know what to make of this happening. After the Priest observed this for a little while, he said he had to return to his Parish Rectory. Patricia, her sister, and the other six ladies present yet and observing this water dripping from only Jesus one middle toe, kept watching. Three ladies had emptied water bottles and began to collect the water drops in their bottles. The three ladies collecting the drops of water smelled the water they had collected, and passed their containers around for ladies to smell. The water collected smelled of a beautiful floral perfume type smell, not like any smell any of them or Patricia had ever smelled before. Everyone smelling this was in awe, thinking this was a miracle thanking us for being there to pray for an end to abortion. Patricia did not have a bottle to collect these water drops, and asked one lady while she was continuing to collect these water drops (that were coming at a very slow pace), if she could put her rosary she used to pray with there under the water drops, and this lady said, sure, OK. Patricia took her Holy Rosary out of her pocket and put it under the water drops. Within 15 seconds or less, the water drops started coming out so fast, much more rapidly, that it didn't take long to drench Patricia's Holy Rosary with these precious perfumed smelling water drops. The other ladies immediately responded, look how fast the water drops are now coming out on her rosary. Patricia started to cry, knowing God was showing his appreciation of the prayers of the Priest and those present praying along.

Soon thereafter, one of the ladies with her little container asked if I would move my rosary so she could collect the faster water drops now and fill up her container more rapidly. Patricia said "Yes", that's fine, and removed her holy rosary drenched in water; and, this rosary is very special to her, and she continues to use very often. When this lady put her small bottle to collect these drops at a faster pace now, within less than 15 seconds, the water drops went back to their normal slow pace. The ladies were in awe at this change in back to slow drops again, as was Patricia, but they still collected water at a slow pace.

Picture of the beautiful large Crucifix near by the Abortion Clinic

Miraculous Picture of Blue Monstrance In The Perpetual Eucharistic Adoration Chapel as Patricia Saw It

2013/09/

PICTURE APPEARING OUTER CIRCLE OF THE MONSTRANCE BEING "<u>RED IN COLOR</u>" AND THE EUCHARISTIC CONSECRATED HOST APPEARS A "<u>DARKER COLOR RED</u>". THIS SHOWED PATRICIA THE PRESENCE OF THE PRECIOUS BODY AND BLOOD OF JESUS CHRIST IN THE EUCHARISTIC CONSECRATED HOST. ALSO, NOTICE THE BACKGROUND DARKER SHADES OF BLUE BEHIND THE RED MONSTRANCE WHICH COLOR IS NOT ON THE PICTURE OF THE ORIGINAL BLUE MONSTRANCE, AS THAT COLOR BACKGROUND IS "<u>LIGHT BROWN OAK.</u>" <u>ALSO, TO NOTE IS THAT THE RED MONSTRANCE MIRACULOUSLY APPEARED ON THE BLUE MONSTRANCE PICTURE ON PATRICIA'S COMPUTER SCREEN. PATRICIA ASKED JESUS WHY THE DARK BLUE BEHIND THE RED MONSTRANCE. JESUS RESPONDED, "IT'S BECAUSE THE SKIES BECAME DARK WHEN I DIED ON THE CROSS.</u>

*** This is the Rosary used by Patricia at the LARGE Crucifix site.
This Rosary was blessed by a Catholic Priest**

The following day, Patricia returned to this site of the beautiful large Crucifix to see if Jesus middle toe was still dripping water drops, and it was no longer dripping water drops. Patricia treasured this Holy Miracle, especially the water drops from Jesus one middle toe coming out so much faster over her Holy Rosary. Sometime soon thereafter, while Patricia was in her home Catholic Church Eucharistic Perpetual Adoration Chapel, and after praying for a while, Patricia sat down. She started to ask Jesus Christ a couple of questions she was hoping to receive an answer from Jesus. Patricia asked "Why was just his middle toe on one of his feet on the Crucifix nearby the Clinic doing abortions the only toe dripping drops of water; and, why did the water drops have this beautiful floral/perfume type scent, unlike any scent any of us ladies present had ever smelled before?" Within a few seconds, Patricia received an interior message answer from Jesus. Jesus told Patricia that the center toe dripping water meant the third toe in from either side of his five toes on the foot, representing three, the Blessed Trinity, three in one, God the Father, God the Son, and God the Holy Spirit. Jesus further explained to Patricia, that the floral/perfume smell of the water drops was because when he was having dinner at the home of Lazarus, Martha and Mary, Mary took perfumed oil to anoint his feet, and then dried his feet with her hair. Patricia then gave thanks to Jesus in Perpetual Adoration for giving her this insight on what the miracle she witnessed a few days earlier at his crucifix. Patricia shared the miracle with the Catholic Priest who leads the prayers every Saturday; she also shared this miracle in writing to many Catholic Priests, her Archdiocese Archbishop, some of her friends and a few relatives.

4.

The first picture showed when Patricia backed up a little to take that picture of "Our Lady of Perpetual Help" to include the whole Shrine area with the candles lit and the flowers there. To Patricia, this picture was another **miracle**, this huge body of light, like **a white cloud in even proportions** with a glow of gold yellow on the border surrounding the picture. The actual picture of "Our Lady of Perpetual Help" it self, **is not** actually seen very well at all, but Patricia feels this was not a flash of any kind. "And then they will see the 'Son of Man coming in the clouds' with great power and glory, and then he will send out the angels and gather [his] elect from the four winds, from the end of the earth to the end of the sky." **Mk 13: 26-27.**

5.

The other picture of Our **Lady of Perpetual Help** was taken at a close up range as it is seen by Patricia.

SHRINE TO "OUR LADY OF PERPETUAL HELP"

PATRICIA'S FIRST PICTURE OF <u>"OUR LADY OF PERPETUAL HELP"</u> (WHEN SHE BACKED UP TO TAKE A PICTURE OF THE WHOLE SHRINE AREA) NOTICE, ONE CAN HARDLY SEE HER PICTURE AT ALL ABOVE THE FLOWERS IN THE CENTER. PATRICIA NOTED LITTLE GOLD CIRCLES AROUND THE FLOWER'S ALL OVER, IN THE CANDLES AND ON TOP OF THE CANDLES. TO PATRICIA, THIS IMAGE IS DEFINITELY A MIRACULOUS PICTURE OF THE BLESSED VIRGIN MARY, WITH THE BEAUTIFUL YELLOW AROUND A WHITE CLOUD; AND, IN PERFECT FORMATION. ALSO THE YELLOW REFLECTION OFF ON THE TWO SIDE WALLS OF THE SHRINE AREA IS VERY NICE.

A CLOSE-UP PICTURE OF "OUR LADY OF PERPETUAL HELP" IN THE SHRINE AREA

UPDATES

6. January 13, 2009 Update

Patricia had submitted her book for publishing with a publishing company that didn't work out for her the latter part of September, 2008, which all the materials she submitted were returned to her soon. She had a miracle occur for her in November, 2008 when she asked Saint Padre Pio of Pietrelcina's help to intercede to God for her in prayer in a nine-day novena. PATRICIA had been in the fourth day of this novena to Saint Padre Pio about this publishing firm; and, she was sad as things didn't seem to be working out for her. In that afternoon at **3:00 pm.** she lied down to rest and was going to pray The Chaplet of Divine Mercy. She also has a Rosary CD of the Joyful, Sorrowful and Glorious Mysteries of the Rosary, but it **was not** in her small CD/radio player. All of a sudden, the **Sorrowful Mysteries** started up and she decided she was meant to pray along with them and felt so different, kind of like she was very, very devout, and in a different world so to speak. Then the **Glorious Mysteries** followed and came on and she prayed along with those also, and the conclusion prayers that included, **The Litany of Loreto.** She felt at utter peace praying. When this was done, she got up and looked in her CD/radio player; this Rosary CD was not in the player, and the radio/CD player was not even on. She thanked Saint Padre Pio for giving her this experience; she knew it was his hearing her intercessory prayers to him that started up the Sorrowful mysteries of the Rosary at the time Jesus died on the Cross, at 3:00 pm. in the afternoon. Saint Padre Pio, at this time, gave Patricia confidence to continue to move on, and a feeling of perseverance.

7. September 3, 2013 Update

On September 3, Patricia was praying the ninth day of her novena to Saint Padre Pio.

On September 3, 2013, as Patricia was editing this book (Patricia had been sick for quite a while; and, in the past few months, she has been editing her book). As Patricia was going through her book and the pictures she has in this book, she noticed that the Holy Monstrance that was this beautiful blue color, had once before been placed in her book; the second picture in the page following the picture of the large crucifix. Then on September 3, 2013, she decided that maybe it was not necessary to have this picture in the book twice. As she highlighted this beautiful blue Monstrance, she tried to delete this picture; then, the Holy Monstrance suddenly appeared in this beautiful red color (the outer part that was in blue) and the Consecrated Host was in a darker red color. She was in awe! She proceeded to make the sign of the

cross over it on her computer screen. She praised and thanked God, Jesus, and The Holy Spirit. She tried saving the picture, but could not, as it didn't work to save it. She clicked on the picture, and the Monstrance went back to blue. She once again tried highlighting the picture to see if this beautiful red monstrance with the darker color red of the Consecrated Host would be there again; it <u>did</u> come again as red (the same as above in this paragraph). She took a picture of it with her camera so she could place that picture in her photo gallery on the computer. Patricia says this happened on the ninth day of a nine day novena of prayers to St. Padre Pio of Pietrelcina to intercede in prayer for her to God for continued assistance in her manuscript. Patricia prayed then to St. Padre Pio to thank him for these prayers for her in seeking God's assistance, as she always thanks him, other saints, and The Blessed Virgin Mary, Queen of all saints, for their intercessory prayers to God on her behalf. St. Padre Pio suffered the stigmata (wounds of Christ at his crucifixion). Patricia says she will be in awe and in love with this red monstrance picture always, as she is with the blue monstrance. **Patricia believes the darker color RED Eucharistic Consecrated Host shows the true presence of the body and blood of Jesus Christ present in the Blessed Sacrament.** <u>****Patricia asked Jesus why the back part behind the red monstrance was a very dark blue, instead of light brown oak color. Jesus said to her: "It's because the skies were dark when I died on the cross.</u>"

<u>JOHN, CHAPTER 20; 24-29</u>

Thomas, called Didymus, one of the Twelve, was not with them when Jesus came. So the other disciples said to him, "We have seen the Lord." But he said to them, "Unless I see the mark of the nails in his hands and put my finger into the "nailmarks" and put my hand into his side, I will not believe." Now a week later his disciples were again inside and Thomas was with them. Jesus came, although the doors were locked, and stood in their midst and said, "Peace be with you." Then he said to Thomas, "Put your finger here and see my hands, and bring your hand and put it into my side, and do not be unbelieving, but believe." Thomas answered and said to him, "My Lord and my God! Jesus said to him, "Have you come to believe because you have seen me? Blessed are those who have not seen and have believed."

<u>RECOMMENDATIONS BY PATRICIA</u>

Patricia is recommending, through God's direction, to pray these prayers nine days in succession, and if a day is forgotten or missed, to continue with the next day they missed. Also, God wanted to dedicate these nine days of prayer for a typical nine-month pregnancy to pray for an end to abortion. These prayers can be prayed any time throughout the year individually; and, in group prayer, at homes, or in church.

Note: Day nine (9) of these prayers, can be said nine (9) days in a row for those who are not Christians, but believe in GOD.

Christians who don't believe in the intercessory prayers of the Blessed Virgin Mary and the saints, to God for their petitions, can say the first eight days of prayer and substitute God, Jesus and The Holy Spirit; or, The Blessed Trinity. Then they also pray the ninth day of prayer.

Christians who do believe in the intercessory petition prayers through the Blessed Virgin Mary and the saints to God, pray all nine days of prayer.

INTRODUCTION

INTRODUCTION TO PATRICIA, DURING HER FIRST VISIT TO THE EUCHARISTIC PERPETUAL ADORATION CHAPEL WITH HER NOTEBOOK

During the course of her first ten minutes of writing in Perpetual Adoration Chapel of a Roman Catholic Church, she knelt in prayer first on a kneeler, then sat down and got out her notebook. On two visits prior to this, and this day also, the outer (approximate three (3) inches wide,) she saw this beautiful blue color in this evenly designed part of the Holy Monstrance. The center of the monstrance displayed Jesus Large Eucharistic Consecrated Host. Patricia asked God "Why are you asking me to write down this information?" Through an immediate interior locution, God responded:

"You have been my faithful servant for many years, giving me your suffering by uniting it to my Son Jesus suffering on the Holy Cross, immediately following receiving my Son Jesus in "The Holy Eucharist." God further said, "Daughter, you offer your receipt of Jesus in the Holy Eucharist in reparation for the sins of the world and the conversion of sinners back to me." God said: "this is why I am asking you to write this for me." Patricia thanked God for this privilege to do this for God, and his only Son, Jesus Christ and the Holy Spirit, as she gazed upon the Sacred Consecrated Host of Jesus.

GOD'S FURTHER INTERIOR LOCUTION TO PATRICIA

In this prayer book, I, God, would like to start with a new parable about a mustard seed. On the front cover of this prayer book, you see my Mother Mary with my Son Jesus Christ, standing to her side in a field of mustard flowers. She is holding yellow flowers, in full bloom, and tiny seeds coming from those flowers. The yellow seed is very important, as I, God, knew that when this tiny seed was originally planted, it would grow into a full blooming plant. Do you not think I want that seed in a Mother's womb that was conceived, to grow and develop into a full beautiful human baby, given birth to, nurtured and cared for, and above all, loved?

I, God, knew this baby was going to be conceived long before it happened.
I created this person in my image and likeness, to be born, grow to a full human being, even if this person was to be born premature, physically or mentally handicapped in any way, this life is precious to me. This life has a purpose in the world. This person's life has a body and soul, and is alive at the moment of conception. I want the baby to develop in the Mother's womb, given birth to, be raised and living life to the fullest, with all the talents this person will achieve as a full human being. Remember, I want to be the one to call this person home and receive this person into my eternal home forever. This life is short here in this world, why make it shorter by aborting the developing conceived seed willfully? My children, I love all of you. Do not refuse my love by saying no to life, this precious gift from me. The usual term of a pregnancy is nine months, and some babies may come early, some may miscarry, be stillborn or die shortly after birth, and there is a reason for this happening. When this happens, the Mother and Father should keep their faith and trust in me that there is a reason for this occurring. A mother or father may not understand the reason in their lifetime on earth, but will understand in heaven. They need to pray and place this sadness and grief of theirs in my hands. To commemorate the typical nine month pregnancy in the mother's womb, I wish "nine days of prayer for an end to abortion, in which these prayers are to include other informative or persuasive issues that could lead a Mother to having an abortion; and, spiritual direction given for individuals and married couples lives." These prayers **should be said in a loving, caring, and compassionate manner; and, never judgmental towards all people prayed for in these nine days of prayer.** God gave Patricia instructions on how the cover of the book in its totality was to look like. Patricia selected a well known Catholic professional oil painting artist in her area to complete a very large size picture of the Blessed Virgin Mary, with her son Jesus (appearing as a youth) along his Mother's side, standing in a field of mustard flowers.

GOD gave Patricia the title of the book: <u>**Blessed Virgin Mary, Mother Of All Nations, Pray For Us.**</u>

Nine Days of Prayer for an <u>End</u> To Abortion, and other unhealthy Informative issues or persuasions that could relate to a Mother having an Abortion; and Spiritual direction for individuals and married couples lives

<u>CHAPTER ONE</u>
<u>DAY ONE (1) OF PRAYER</u>

<u>**Gen 1: 26-28**</u> Then God said: "Let us make man in our image, after our likeness. Let them have dominion over the fish of the sea, the birds of the air, and the cattle, and over all the wild animals and all the creatures that crawl on the ground."

> God created man in his image;
> in the divine image he created
> him;
> male and female he created them.

God blessed them, saying: "Be fertile and multiply; fill the earth and subdue it. Have dominion over the fish of the sea, the birds of the air, and all the living things that move on the earth."

<u>**Psalm 119: 73**</u> Your hands made me and fashioned
> me;
> give me insight to learn your commands.

<u>**Jer 1: 5**</u> Before I formed you in the womb I
> knew you,
> before you were born I dedicated
> you.

<u>**Luke, 1, 46-55**</u>

And Mary said:

"My soul proclaims the greatness of the Lord;

my spirit rejoices in God my savior.
For he has looked upon his handmaid's
       lowliness;
       behold, from now on will all ages call
          me blessed.
The Mighty One has done great things
       for me,
       and holy is his name.
His mercy is from age to age
       to those who fear him.
He has shown might with his arm,
       dispersed the arrogant of mind and
          heart.
He has thrown down the rulers from
          their thrones
       but lifted up the lowly.
The hungry he has filled with good
          things;
       the rich he has sent away empty.
He has helped Israel his servant,
       remembering his mercy,
according to his promise to our fathers,
       to Abraham and to his descendants
          forever."

Proverbs 4: 8-9
Extol her, and she will exalt you;
       She will bring you honors if you embrace her;
She will put on your head a graceful
          diadem;
       a glorious crown will she bestow on you.

John 19: 26-27
When Jesus saw his mother and the disciple there whom he loved, he said to his mother, "Woman, behold your son." Then he said to the disciple, "Behold, your mother."

I Timothy 2: 1-4
First of all, then, I ask that supplications, prayers, petitions, and thanksgivings be offered for everyone, for kings and for all in authority, that we may lead a quiet

and tranquil life in all devotion and dignity. This is good and pleasing to God, our savior, who wills everyone to be saved and to come to knowledge of the truth.

My God, I love thee. God, I thank you for the precious gift of life. Dear God, help mothers and fathers all over the world to realize this precious gift. Lord, give them strength, courage and determination to carry their conceived child in the mother's womb and to give birth to the baby. Holy God, I ask that people seek HOLINESS, PRAYER, PEACE, FAITH, HOPE, TRUST and LOVE in their lives.

I praise and worship you God! In you, LORD, I place my hope! I pray, Dear God, for an end to abortion in this world, done by abortion doctors, their assistants and nurses who assist in abortion procedures. In addition, there is wrong advice given to a mother by pro-choice advocates. I pray, Lord, for women to realize that an abortion may be harmful to them; and, they too, could have injuries and/or die from the procedure.

Lord, I pray for people responsible in any way for these murders of innocent little conceived babies in the mother's womb, for them to express deep sorrow for these sins, and seek your forgiveness. Dear Lord, help these people to not believe in or perform abortions, and to seek a new and holy mission with a firm resolve to amend their lives, where they will find holiness and peace, which is good for their souls.

Dear God, may your Son Jesus Sacred Heart give his blessing of conversion, love, and holiness to the hearts of people involved in legalizing abortions, in performing or assisting in abortions, nurses who assist in abortion procedures,, and pro-choice advocates, to change and become pro-life advocates. Dear God I pray, that these people say: **"No to the Prince of all evil, the Father of all lies, the Devil, also known as Satan,"** who loves to get more disobedient souls. **I pray, in your name Lord, that Satan leave their hearts and minds, and that you, Lord, convert them to what is holy and perfect for their souls; and, respecting the sanctity of life.**

I pray, Lord, that people understand that believing in or approving of abortions are **wrong** in saying: "It's a woman's right or choice to kill the little innocent babies from conception and up to partial birth abortions." Dear God, help women to know that "**it is not a woman's right to kill these precious conceived babies as every life is known to you.**" "With all my ways you are familiar." **(Psalm 139:3)**. "Before I formed you in the womb I knew you." **(Jer. 1:5)**.

I pray, Lord, help us to know that The Blessed Trinity is pure, your Holy Mother Mary is pure, and we are to seek to be pure. I pray we think of the color **"white"** as to think of the **dove** which is white and depicts **The Holy Spirit**, who is pure. I know, Lord, that we are all sinners, and that the Blessed Virgin Mary was conceived without sin, in her "Immaculate Conception." Dear Lord Jesus, I pray people don't act lustfully in outside of marriage acts of sex, swinger groups, incest, prostitution, fornication, etc. I pray, Jesus, people should realize that these activities often are against the possible life of the conceived child with abortions and abortifacient drugs being used, such as the RU-486 pill; and, are **against two of your ten (10) commandments, "You shall not kill;" "you shall not commit adultery." Exo 20: 13-14.**

Dearest Jesus, you said: ***"I am the way and the truth and the life" Jn. 14: 6.*** Dear God, you knew when we were conceived in our Mother's womb, and that you wanted us to be born and to live our lives to the fullest serving and loving you. I pray God, people understand that you want to save souls, and choose the time they are born into this world; and, the time they come home to you in heaven for everlasting peace, joy, and love. I love, adore, praise, worship, and give you thanks, my Lord and Savior, Jesus Christ.

Dear Blessed Virgin Mary, loving and merciful Mother of All Nations, please give your motherly help to all mother's who in wanting an abortion, that you pray to God for them not to have an abortion; you are very saddened by abortions, as is The Blessed Trinity. I pray, Blessed Virgin Mary, you inspire them with your motherly love to their hearts that there is help for them at Pro-life Centers. May Our Jesus of Divine Mercy, have mercy on mothers who have had an abortion and forgive those who have died from the procedure.

Sacred Heart of Jesus, through your protection and the protection of your Holy Mother Mary's Immaculate Heart, protect all pro-life centers set up around the world for the protection of mothers and the infants growing in their wombs, to save more and more lives each day. We pray, Dear God, politicians and Supreme Court officials, who legalize abortion around the world, have a change of heart to make all abortions, the RU-486 morning after pill, or other abortifacient drugs illegal. I pray, Dear Jesus and Blessed Mother Mary that these centers stay safe from abortion advocates and always continue to grow to help mothers and the infant growing in their wombs. Dearest St. Joseph, Foster Father of Jesus and most chaste spouse of Our Blessed Virgin Mary, I pray for your intercession in prayer and blessings from your carpentry experience, more pro-life centers are built all over the world. I pray, Dearest Blessed Virgin Mary, through your intercessory prayers to God, that positive advice is always given at these pro-life centers. I pray, dear Mother Mary that people realize women should be given advice on **natural family planning.**

I pray, Dear Jesus, that our youth, young women and women of the world realize the dangers of taking contraceptives and abortifacient drugs, such as the RU-486 pill. I pray, Jesus, they read the warning labels on the paperwork that comes with these drugs. I pray, Dear Jesus, they realize contraceptive use can cause breast cancer, cervix cancer and liver cancer; and other illnesses. I pray, Dear Jesus, ladies who take abortifacient drugs realize that they are at risk for heavy bleeding, serious pain and complications, and will need to seek a doctor. I pray, Jesus, they realize the risks of any abortion procedure and this emotional loss in their lives.

I pray, Dear Lord that birth control pills, the morning/day after pill RU-486, or possibly abortifacient drugs, are never available at schools, and colleges; and, never recommended by the parents of children in their age of youth or young adulthood to use. I pray, Lord, that these young people to not give in to pressure because their peers are having sex. I pray, Lord, that parent's monitor their children's activities such as: doing bad things on the internet that may get them mixed up with pimps, or meeting the wrong kind of people that could kidnap, rape, harm, or kill them; also, pornography web sites, and to know if their daughter may be on birth control pills. I pray, Dear God that teens, young adults and adults are aware that if they are on the birth control pill, they should never be confused to also take the RU-486 morning after pill, which could harm them. We pray that pro-choice centers or pro-choice advocates never recommend the use of the RU-486 pill, or to have an abortion.

I worship you Jesus! I pray, Blessed Virgin Mary, for you to intercede with me in prayer to **God for pro-choice people to convert their hearts to your son Jesus Sacred Heart, and no longer believe in abortion.** I pray, Dear Jesus, that this slaughter of the **"innocents"** comes to an end, and that these precious **"innocents"** have their chance to live their lives here on earth, having a loving, caring and productive life; and, that they go home to be with God when **GOD** calls them.

I pray Jesus, that people understand that <u>you would never be pro-choice regarding abortions, approve that mothers have an abortion; or, for abortionists, their assistants, and nurses to perform abortions.</u>

I pray, Dear God, that all people who believe in you, take time in their <u>lives</u> to spend at least 15 to 30 minutes daily in quiet prayer in their own rooms or a quiet place of prayer for them; that in their prayers to you, they <u>**"pause and listen"; and, understand they can have loving communication with you, Almighty God.**</u>

Blessed Virgin Mary, Mother of all nations, pray for us.

Romans, Chapter 12: 2; 9-12
Ch 12: 2; 9-12

Do not conform yourself to this age but be transformed by the renewal of your mind, that you may discern what is the will of God, what is good and pleasing and perfect. Let love be sincere; hate what is evil, hold on to what is good; love one another with mutual affection; anticipate one another in showing honor. Do not grow slack in zeal, be fervent in spirit, serve the Lord. Rejoice in hope, endure in affliction, persevere in prayer.

Psalm 32: 1-5

Happy the sinner whose fault is removed,
    whose sin is forgiven.
Happy those to whom the LORD imputes
      no guilt,
  in whose spirit is no deceit
As long as I kept silent, my bones
      wasted away;
    I groaned all the day.
For day and night your hand was heavy upon me;
    my strength withered as in dry summer heat.
Then I declared my sin to you;
    my guilt I did not hide.
I said, "I confess my faults to the LORD,"
    and you took away the guilt of my sin.

Psalm 51: 5; 58: 3; 127: 3; 128: 4

51:5 For I know my offense;
      my sin is always before me.
58:3 No, you freely engage in crime;
      your hands dispense violence to the earth.
127:3 Children too are a gift from the LORD,
      the fruit of the womb, a reward.
128:4 Just so will they be blessed
      who fear the LORD.

1 Cor, 11: 23-29; 31

For I received from the Lord what I also handed on to you, that the Lord Jesus, on the night he was handed over, took bread, and, after he had given thanks, broke it and said, "This is my body that is for you. Do this in remembrance of me." In the same way also the cup, after supper, saying, "This cup is the new covenant in my blood. Do this, as often as you drink it, in remembrance of me."

For as often as you eat this bread and drink the cup, you proclaim the death of the Lord until he comes.

Therefore whoever eats the bread or drinks the cup of the Lord unworthily will have to answer for the body and blood of the Lord. A person should examine himself, and so eat the bread and drink the cup. For anyone who eats and drinks without discerning the body, eats and drinks judgment on himself. If we discerned ourselves, we would not be under judgment.

CHAPTER II
DAY TWO (2) OF PRAYER

Psalm 119: 73; 139: 13; Jer. 1: 4-5

119: 73 Your hands made me and fashioned me;
give me insight to learn your commands.

139: 13 You formed my inmost being:
you knit me in my mother's womb.
Jer. 1: 4-5
The word of the LORD came to me thus:
Before I formed you in the womb I knew you.
before you were born, I dedicated you,
a prophet to the nations I appointed you.

I thank you God for the gift of life and all your abundant blessings and graces! Jesus, I love you! Holy Spirit, I praise you and I love you!

Jesus, Our Savior, and Blessed Mother Mary, I pray with you to intercede to God for the protection and blessings upon all Pro-life advocates, their centers for pro-life, and any pro-life hospitals or organizations set up for pro-life protection of the baby conceived in the Mother's womb. *Jesus, Our Savior, and Blessed Mother Mary,* I pray for your protection and blessings upon all pro-life advocate groups; and, that in the protests of the pro-life and pro-choice advocate groups against each other, I pray that no harm comes to either of these groups. I pray, *Dear Lord Jesus,* that pro-life and pro-choice advocates establish a covenant of unity and peace together, to end the evils of abortion. Dear Jesus, please help them indulge their efforts in unity to raise funds to build more pro-life centers to help expectant mothers and fathers.

I Cor, 1: 10 "I urge you, brothers, in the name of our Lord Jesus Christ, that all of you agree in what you say, and that there be no divisions among you, but that you be united in the same and in the same purpose."
Jesus, My Savior and Redeemer, I pray for protection of the conceived unborn child in the Mother's womb. Dearest Jesus, you said: **"Do to others whatever you would have them do to you. This is the law and the prophets."** **Matthew, 7: 12.** *Dearest Jesus,* I pray abortionists, their assistants, nurses and pro-choice advocates realize the **seriousness of this HOLY underlined bible passage made above in this paragraph, especially if they came in harms way; for instance, if they were under need of serious medical attention, or an attack on them witnessed by someone else, etc.?** I pray, Jesus, to help them to recognize the unborn child in the mother's womb that is squirming and **suffering** for their lives when abortion procedures are done, when they were content on sucking their thumbs and moving around. We pray, Lord, in third trimester abortions and the baby is born alive, that this life be placed in an incubator, hopefully saved, and not killed. I pray, Dearest Jesus, they examine their own consciences and decide, would this be the kind of **example or role model** they want to pass off to their own children, if they have children, grandchildren or great grandchildren. Dearest Jesus, help them to understand, that their own children live by their **"example" or role model.** Dearest Mother Mary, I pray with you for your intercessory help to God, for all the people involved in legalizing abortion, abortionists, their assistants, nurses, and pro-choice advocates; I pray they amend their lives, change to pro-life, repent of these **sins,** and seek your Son Jesus merciful forgiveness. I pray. Lord, that they seek emotional healing (through individual or group therapy, or a retreat center for this purpose).

Dearest Lord, I pray that women who have experienced an abortion, taking the RU-486 morning after pill, or other abortifacient drugs, that there is personal healing to themselves for having had used any of these procedures. I pray, Dear Jesus, that they seek (as well as the father) counseling (therapy) and or group therapy. I pray, Lord, they should pray their Holy Bibles/Holy Books of prayer to help them. May this, renew their faith, hope, and trust back to God in their lives.

I pray, Holy Spirit, for you to illuminate and renew your seven gifts, especially your gifts of **knowledge, fear of the LORD, fortitude and counsel** to pro-choice lawmakers, pro-choice advocates, abortionists, their assistants, and nurses involved in abortion procedures; and, mothers, and fathers who want an abortion. I pray, Holy Spirit that these people realize abortion, the RU-486 morning after pill and other abortifacient drugs are very wrong and evil. I pray, Holy Spirit, they amend their lives, realizing that what they are doing as being very offensive to God; and, change these evil, immoral, and unhealthy attitude/ideas in their hearts and minds to pro-life. Holy Spirit, heal them! I pray, Dear Holy Spirit, a mother and father realize their child is **created in God's image and likeness**. May they also realize, Holy Spirit, **God knew they were going to be conceived long before it happened; and,** to have their right to life, and having whatever goals, aspirations, and joy to achieve in their lives.

Holy Spirit, I pray proper **counsel** is always given to the youth of the world. Holy Spirit, instill your gifts of **knowledge, counsel, and fear of the Lord** to junior and high schools, government authority officials, that this is wrong and immoral to provide contraceptives or abortifacient drugs to our youth; and, often, without the consent or knowledge of the parents. We pray, Holy Spirit, they realize that this often encourages promiscuous behavior and adultery. **Holy Spirit, I pray that you heal these people and our youth of the world,** instilling purity and holiness in their hearts and minds; and, give them the advice of prayer in their daily lives, especially "The Lord's Prayer" **Matt, Ch 6: 9-13**. Holy Spirit, I pray that young teenage girls, if they get pregnant, to tell their parents about their pregnancy; and, their parents provide help to a pro-life center for them. I pray, *Dear God, Our Lord,* full of mercy and love for all of us, that in acknowledging ourselves as sinners, as we are all sinners, that I can give your mercy, love, and forgiveness to others.

Blessed Virgin Mary, Mother of all nations, pray for us.

Psalm 31: 2-5, 25

In you, LORD, I take refuge;
    let me never be put to shame.
In your justice deliver me;
    incline your ear to me;
    make haste to rescue me!
Be my rock of refuge,
    a stronghold to save me.
You are my rock and my fortress;
    for your name's sake lead and guide me.
Free me from the net they have set for me,
    for you are my refuge.

Be strong and take heart;
    all you who hope in the LORD.

Phil. 1: 8-11

For God is my witness, how I long for all of you with the affection of Christ Jesus. And this is my prayer: that your love may increase ever more and more in knowledge and every kind of perception, to discern what is of value, so that you may be pure and blameless for the day of Christ, filled with the fruit of righteousness that comes through Jesus Christ for the glory and praise of God.

Colossians, 3: 12-17

Put on then, as God's chosen ones, holy and beloved, heartfelt compassion, kindness, humility, gentleness, and patience, bearing with one another and forgiving one another, if one has a grievance against another; as the Lord has forgiven you, so must you also do. And over all these put on love, that is, the bond of perfection. And let the peace of Christ control your hearts, the peace into which you were also called in one body. And be thankful. Let the word of Christ dwell in you richly, as in all wisdom you teach and admonish one another, singing psalms, hymns, and spiritual songs with gratitude in your hearts to God. And whatever you do, in word or in deed, do everything in the name of the Lord Jesus, giving thanks to God the Father through him.

Ephesians, 4: 1-6; 20-27; 32; 5: 15-17

I, then, a prisoner for the Lord, urge you to live in a manner worthy of the call you have received, with all humility and gentleness, with patience, bearing with one another through love, striving to preserve the unity of the spirit through the bond of peace: one body and one Spirit, as you were also called to the one hope of your call; one Lord, one faith, one baptism; one God and Father of all, who is over all and through all and in all.

That is not how you learned Christ, assuming that you have heard of him and were taught in him, as truth is in Jesus, that you should put away the old self of your former way of life, corrupted through deceitful desires, and be renewed in the spirit of your minds, and put on the new self, created in God's way in righteousness and holiness of truth.

Therefore, putting away falsehood, speak the truth, each one to his neighbor, for we are members one of another. Be angry, but do not sin; do not let the sun set on your anger, and do not leave room for the devil. [And] be kind to one another, compassionate, forgiving one another as God has forgiven you in Christ.

Ephesians 5: 15-17
15 Watch carefully then how you live, not as foolish persons but as wise, making the most of the opportunity, because the days are evil. Therefore, do not continue in ignorance, but try to understand what is the will of the Lord.

CHAPTER 3
DAY THREE (3) OF PRAYER

Psalm 51: 3-6, 9-14
Have mercy on me, God, in your goodness;
in your abundant compassion blot out my offense.
Wash away all my guilt;
from my sin cleanse me.
For I know my offense;
my sin is always before me.
Against you alone have I sinned;
I have done such evil in your sight
That you are just in your sentence,
blameless when you condemn.

Cleanse me with hyssop, that I may be pure;
wash me, make me whiter than snow.
Let me hear sounds of joy and gladness;
let the bones you have crushed rejoice.

Turn away your face from my sins;
blot out all my guilt.

A clean heart create for me, God;
renew in me a steadfast spirit.
Do not drive me from your presence,
nor take away from me your holy spirit.
Restore my joy in your salvation;
sustain in me a willing spirit.

I praise , adore, worship and love The Blessed Trinity. Dearest Mother Mary, I ask and pray with you for your intercessory help, for all the people involved in legalizing abortion, abortionists, their assistants, nurses, and pro-choice advocates, that they express sorrow for these sins, amend their life, change to pro-life, and seek your Son Jesus merciful forgiveness.

Dear Jesus, your apostle Paul said: "for building up the body of Christ, until we all attain to the unity of faith and knowledge of the Son of God, to mature manhood, to the extent of the full stature of Christ." **Eph, Ch 4: 12-13.**

I pray, Holy Spirit, for you to illuminate and renew your seven gifts, especially your gifts of **knowledge, counsel,** and **fear of the LORD** (of knowing abortion, using the RU 486 morning after pill and other abortifacient drugs, are wrong, immoral, evil, and very offensive to God); and, **fortitude** to pro-choice lawmakers, pro-choice advocates, abortionists, their assistants, and nurses who assist in or perform abortions, and expectant mothers, to amend their lives to prolife. We pray they change immoral and unhealthy attitude/ideas in their hearts and minds to a new wholesome healthy mission respecting all life from conception to birth of a new baby. Holy Spirit, heal them! I pray, Holy Spirit, heal our youth, young adults, and adults of the world, instilling purity and holiness in their hearts and minds; I pray people spend at least 30 minutes a day in prayer to you, saying "The Our Father" prayer, Holy Bibles, or Holy books of prayer. Dearest Lord, I pray women who have experienced an abortion or taking the RU-486 morning after pill, that they seek individual therapy; or, support group therapy and spirituality; and, to repent and seek Jesus merciful forgiveness, as you are always compassionate and loving.

I pray, Jesus, ,through the intercessory prayers of your Holy Mother Mary, that birth control pills, the RU-486 morning after pill, or other abortifacient drugs are never given out at middle schools, junior high schools, and high schools for the young girls and women to use. I Pray, Dear Lord Jesus, that a young girl in her youth, young women, and adult women never attempt to do their own abortion procedure, as this could result in serious injuries, infections, bleeding or death.

I pray, Dear Jesus, and through the intercessory prayers with us of your Mother, the

Blessed Virgin Mary, as she loves and cares for the well being of all your children on earth as you do; and, the hearts and minds of possible evil happenings, that mothers and fathers **are converted to goodness. I pray, God, that they not take** illegal drugs and other (often homemade) drugs, and have very strict limitations in drinking alcohol; Dear God, instill in their minds, that these drugs and drinking too much alcohol (especially being dangerous in driving their vehicles), are very wrong and harmful for peoples use in their lives; and, often causing addictions, and some people overdosing on drugs. Jesus, I pray, that mother's be made aware that if they are pregnant, that could cause: **harm to the fetus/fetuses growing in a mother's womb, babies having to go through many other medical issues that will happen to the infant growing in the mother's womb, such as fetal alcohol syndrome (FAS); withdrawal, and brain or physical damage to their precious baby's bodies. I pray, Dear Jesus, they realize their child may be born stillborn; and, mother's may miscarry the child, or she may decide to abort the child (she figuring it will be born handicapped or very ill at birth) while on these drugs and alcohol.** We pray, Dear Lord, Our God of love, full of mercy and compassion for all your children, they all are given the Holy Spirits gifts of **counsel, fortitude and knowledge** to acknowledge what is good for the physical and mental well-being of the mother, and her child growing in her womb.

Blessed Virgin Mary, Mother of all nations, pray for us.

Wisdom, 1: 3-6

For perverse counsels separate a man from God,
    and his power, put to the proof, rebukes the foolhardy;
Because into a soul that plots evil wisdom enters not,
    nor dwells she in a body under debt of sin.
For the holy spirit of discipline flees deceit
    and withdraws from senseless counsels;
    and when injustice occurs, it is rebuked
For wisdom is a kindly spirit,
    yet she acquaints not the blasphemer of his guilty lips;
Because God is the witness of his inmost self
    and the sure observer of his heart
    and the listener to his tongue.

Matthew 18: 6-7

Whoever causes one of these little ones who believe in me to sin, it would be better for him to have a great millstone hung around his neck and to be drowned in the depths of the sea. Woe to the world because of things that cause sin!

CHAPTER FOUR (4)

DAY FOUR (4) OF PRAYER

Psalm 30: 2-4; 119: 73

I praise you, LORD, for you raised me up
   and did not let my enemies rejoice over me.
O LORD, my God,
   I cried out to you and you healed me.
LORD, you brought me up from Sheol;
   you kept me from going down to the pit."

119: 73   Your hands made me and fashioned me;
              give me insight to learn your commands.

All praise, glory and honor to you God My Father! I adore you Jesus! I praise you Holy Spirit! Jesus, I thank you for your Divine Mercy. God, My Father, I thank you for your graces and blessings!

My Dear Lord, many women who live in uttermost poverty and in poor countries, still choose to give birth to their babies. Dear Lord, these women care for their children the best way they can, and often have very little means to do so, but they know their faith in you God will help see them through their caring, nurturing and loving them. Dear God, help all mothers-to-be to have faith and trust in you to carry their child; and, may these children live their life to the fullest to love and serve you. Help mothers and fathers, Dear God, to know their child is precious in your eyes and is a precious gift from you; that if this child would be born handicapped in any way, and, if so, they keep the child. Dear God, we pray that mother's are not injured physically, have an infection, or die from an abortion. We pray, Dear God, that if mothers are injured at these abortion mills from an abortion, that they seek emergency medical care at a hospital. Dear Lord, we also know mothers are injured emotionally after an abortion, and we pray they seek out psychological, (whether private therapists or group therapy); and pray to You Lord, for emotional healing

I pray, Dear God, that parents, husbands or boyfriends who are forcing the mother to have an abortion, realize that this is evil and wrong. I pray, Dear God, when these individuals who are involved in giving abortion advice telling the mother to go ahead and proceed with the abortion, they need to take a second look at their own lives, and be thankful to their parents for giving birth to them.

I pray, Lord, that the above people and any people in government and political decision making involvement around the world, amend their lives, convert their hearts and souls back to you God; I pray that they stop doing or approving these death seeking procedures on a conceived child in the mother's womb. I pray, God, they understand the conceived child's right to their life, as God gives this child the right to live and serve him. **<u>Dear God, you said:</u>**

"Court not death by your erring way of life,
nor draw to yourselves destruction by the works of your hands.
Because God did not make death,
nor does he rejoice in the destruction of the living." **<u>Wisdom 1: 12-13</u>**

I pray to you, Blessed Virgin Mary, to intercede with me in prayer to God for these people, and that when they have difficulty making this choice to stop doing or approving these procedures, they should look at and venerate a picture or statue of you, dear Mother Mary; and, realize that you said **<u>"Yes to God, when he asked you to be the Mother of Our Savior, Jesus Christ;</u> your precious son who suffered and died for our sins, so that we might be saved."** I pray, Dear Blessed Virgin Mary, Our Merciful and Holy Mother, that in your intercessory prayers with me to God, that any type of abortion procedures comes to an end. **<u>We pray, Mother Mary, that women realize that it's "not a woman's choice to have an abortion."</u>** I ask in intercessory prayer with you, Blessed Virgin Mary, to help these people amend their lives, to convert their hearts and souls back to God, and stop immediately their belief in, and abortion procedures; and, to express sorrow and seek forgiveness from Our Merciful God.

Blessed Virgin Mary, Mother of all nations, pray for us, and for the protection of the conceived unborn child. I pray, Mother Mary, that you connect your Immaculate Heart to the hearts of all people who perform abortions, assist in abortion procedures, those in political authority around the world that legalize abortion, and pro-choice advocates; I pray, they convert their **hearts to yours; and, that you wrap your Motherly Mantle of love, care, protection and conversion around them.** I pray, Mother Mary, that you give these intercessory prayers to the Blessed Trinity, seeking conversion of them to your Son Jesus Sacred Heart, Who is full of love and mercy for them. I pray, Mother Mary, that they place their faith, hope and trust in Jesus to help them amend their lives; and, seeking a new holy mission and belief system to pro-life, to repent of their previous thoughts and actions, and to seek Jesus' merciful forgiveness. Mother Mary, I pray you teach them that Jesus said: **"I am the way and the truth and the life,"** <u>**Jn 14: 6**</u> and that they **"Do whatever he tells you."** <u>**Jn 2: 5.**</u> I pray, Mother Mary, under your title, **"Our Lady of Guadalupe",** pray for the protection of the unborn from any harm.

My dearest Jesus, you are known as "Our Jesus of Divine Mercy." Jesus, Our Savior and Redeemer, bless and protect the conceived unborn child. Dearest Jesus, you said, <u>**"Do to others whatever you would have them do to you."**</u> **Mt. 7: 12.** We pray, Jesus, abortionists understand how they would feel if their own mother had aborted them; they being like the unborn child in the mother's womb, that is squirming and **suffering** for their lives from abortion procedures. I pray, Jesus, to help them understand how they would feel if a daughter of theirs didn't tell them about having an abortion. We pray, Jesus, for abortionists to understand as conceived little ones are taken out by suction in a tube, out piece by piece, saline abortions, and wondering what's happening to them in **their pain**; and, all of this pure torture, when they were content in sucking their thumbs, moving around and kicking in their mother's womb. Dearest Jesus, I pray for these people to change to pro-life, as they would appreciate others praying for them to change; and, you directed us **"To love one another, as I have loved you."** I pray, Dear Jesus, if **anyone** involved in approving abortions, doing abortions, assisting in abortions, nurses, and pro-choice people, realize that when **we love one another as you love us; that this means loving the infant growing in the mother's womb from conception, and, not to abort the infant.** Dear Jesus, you also mean these **"in quotes"** statements above for pro-life and pro-choice people in many other facets of their lives also; **"love your enemies, and pray for those who persecute you, that you may be children of your heavenly Father, Mt 5: 44-45"** and **"Blessed are the merciful,/ for they will be shown mercy." Mt 5: 7. Dearest Jesus, St. Paul said in his letter to the Ephesians: "[And] be kind to one another, compassionate, forgiving one another as God has forgiven you in Christ" Eph 4: 32.**

I pray, Dear Jesus, when we repent of our sins, (we all know that we are sinners) we realize your great love, kindness, mercy, peace, and forgiveness of our sins. I pray, Dear Jesus, you send the Holy Spirit upon all of us to help us amend our lives to do what is pleasing, loving and favorable to you, in living our lives in accordance with God's ten (10) commandments. I pray, Dear Jesus, for the following Holy Bible passage to be prayed and instilled in our hearts and souls by the Holy Spirit: **"That is not how you learned Christ, assuming that you have heard of him and were taught in him, as truth is in Jesus, that you should put away the old self of your former way of life, corrupted through deceitful desires, and be renewed in the spirit of your minds, and put on the new self, created in**

God's way in righteousness and holiness of truth." Paul, Eph. 4: 20-24
I praise you Holy Spirit! I pray, Holy Spirit, for you to illuminate and renew your seven gifts; some of these are gifts of **counsel, knowledge** (knowing abortion is murder and a mortal sin), and **fortitude,** (strength to change and amend their lives), upon all people who perform abortions. I pray, Holy Spirit, that you instill **knowledge** in all government political powers in the many areas of the world that pass laws approving abortions, and all who are pro-choice advocates, to convert all of these peoples hearts and minds to pro-life. Amen.

Blessed Virgin Mary, Mother of all nations, pray for us.

Wisdom, Ch 2: 1-5, 22-24

      they who said among themselves, thinking not aright:
"Brief and troublous is our lifetime;
    neither is there any remedy for man's dying,
    nor is anyone known to have come back from the nether world.
For haphazard were we born,
    and hereafter we shall be as though we had not been;
Because the breath in our nostrils is a smoke
    and reason is a spark at the beating of our hearts,
And when this is quenched, our body will be ashes
    and our spirit will be poured abroad like unresisting air.
Even our name will be forgotten in time,
    and no one will recall our deeds.
So our life will pass away like the traces of a cloud,
    and will be dispersed like a mist
    pursued by the sun's rays
    and overpowered by its heat.
For our lifetime is the passing of a shadow;
    and our dying cannot be deferred
    because it is fixed with a seal; and no one returns.

And they knew not the hidden counsels of God;
    neither did they count on a recompense of holiness
    nor discern the innocent souls' reward.
For God formed man to be imperishable;
    the image of his own nature he made him.
But by the envy of the devil, death entered the world,
    and they who are in his possession experience it.

2 CHRON. 7:14

…and if my people, upon whom my name has been pronounced, humble themselves and pray, and seek my presence and turn from their evil ways, I will hear them from heaven and pardon their sins and revive their land.

CHAPTER 5
DAY FIVE (5) OF PRAYER

Psalm 96: 1-3

Sing to the LORD a new song;
    sing to the LORD, all the earth.
Sing to the LORD, bless his name;
    announce his salvation day after day.
Tell God's glory among the nations;
    among all peoples, God's marvelous deeds.

Jeremiah 29: 11-14

For I know well the plans I have in mind for you, says the LORD, plans for your welfare, not for woe! Plans to give you a future full of hope. When you call me, when you go to pray to me, I will listen to you. When you look for me, you will find me. Yes, when you seek me with all your heart, you will find me with you, says the LORD, and I will change your lot.

I praise and worship you, Blessed Trinity! My Dear God, help us to realize that every life is known to you, even before it was conceived, and that you had a divine purpose for this person's life. My Dear God, you knew that life would be conceived and develop in the mother's womb, and would want that child to be born into this world to live their lives to the fullest, loving and serving you. Blessed Virgin Mary, our heavenly mother, who is always here for us to ask her holy intercession to God in prayer; I pray that life is nurtured in the mothers womb, and that the infant is born healthy, and, not aborted. God, we ask that all mothers who have chosen not to give birth and had abortions, that these mothers express true sorrow to you for this mortal sin of abortion, seek your forgiveness, and that you have mercy on them. We pray, Lord, that you bless them, guide them, protect them, and give them strength to endure this loss in their life, and in the life of their spouse or boyfriend. Immaculate Mary, Mother of all Nations, I pray you wrap your Motherly Mantle of love, consolation, care and compassion around all mothers who have experienced an abortion, more than one abortion; or, the use of the RU-486 morning after pill. I pray, that Fathers who have experienced the abortion of a conceived child, that in their sadness and regret of this happening, that you, Blessed Virgin Mary, give them your motherly care, love and consolation.

My God, I pray that additional maternity ward space be provided in hospitals, or if possible, an addition added on to a hospital for maternity space, for mothers to have their babies; and, even when they don't have hospitalization insurance, be given the right to have their child. I pray, Dear Lord, that this could possibly be done through charitable doctors, assistants, and nurses to volunteer to give some time in their day or week, to provide delivery help; or, that these sections in hospitals can be set up by government agencies and staff hired as Federal employees, State or Local government run facilities of this nature. I pray, Lord, that these government employees are paid a comparable salary to that of the private sector for the nature of their work.

Dear Jesus, please bless and give strength and love to the birth mother and or birth parents for giving up their child for adoption; give them faith and hope in knowing that their child will be loved and cared for by the adoptive parents. Dear God, I pray that adoption agencies will have to increase in size, or more opened, to assist in the adoption process for parents who want to adopt a child. Dear God, bless the adoptive parents and give them happiness and thankfulness to you for receiving this child.

Dear Jesus, through your apostle Paul in his letter to the Thessalonians, Paul said: "Pray without ceasing. In all circumstances give thanks, for this is the will of God for you in Christ Jesus. Do not quench the Spirit. Do not despise prophetic utterances. Test everything; retain what is good. Refrain from every kind of evil. May the God of peace himself make you perfectly holy and may you entirely, spirit, soul, and body, be preserved blameless for the coming of our Lord Jesus Christ." **I, Thes. Ch. 5: 17-23**. Dear Jesus, I pray that people "follow you," and always be guided by the Holy Spirit.

Dear Holy Spirit, instill in our hearts and souls, the fires of your love; illuminate us to always do God's will, what is pleasing and holy to God. We pray, Holy Spirit, for you to renew your seven gifts, especially those gifts of **knowledge** (knowing abortion is murder and is a mortal sin) and **fortitude**, (strength to amend their lives). I pray, Holy Spirit, for abortionists, their assistants, nurses who assist in abortions, people in political legal decision making that approve abortion, and all pro-choice advocates; I pray, Holy Spirit, they change these beliefs that abortions are alright to perform, and to convert these people's hearts and minds to pro-life. Amen.

Blessed Virgin Mary, Mother of all nations, pray for us.

I Cor. 11: 27-29
Therefore whoever eats the bread or drinks the cup of the Lord unworthily will have to answer for the body and blood of the Lord. A person should examine himself, and so eat the bread and drink the cup. For anyone who eats and drinks without discerning the body, eats and drinks judgment on himself.

Phil. 1: 8-11
For God is my witness, how I long for all of you with the affection of Christ Jesus. And this is my prayer: that your love may increase ever more and more in knowledge and every kind of perception, to discern what is of value, so that you may be pure and blameless for the day of Christ, filled with the fruit of righteousness that comes through Jesus Christ for the glory and praise of God.

CHAPTER 6
DAY SIX (6) OF PRAYER

Psalm 14: 4-6; Psalm 111: 1-10; Paul, 1 Cor, Ch 2: 9-10

Psalm 14: 4-6
Will these evildoers never learn?
    They devour my people as they devour bread;
    they do not call upon the LORD.
They have good reason, then, to fear;
    God is with the company of the just.
They would crush the hopes of the poor,
    but the poor have the LORD as their refuge.

Psalm 111: 3-10

Majestic and glorious is your work,
    your wise design endures forever.
You won renown for your wondrous deeds;
    gracious and merciful is the LORD.
You gave food to those who fear you,
    mindful of your covenant forever.
You showed powerful deeds to your people,
    giving them the lands of the nations.
The works of your hands are right and true,
    Reliable all your decrees,
Established forever and ever

to be observed with loyalty and care.
You sent deliverance to your people,
   ratified your covenant forever;
   holy and awesome is your name.
The fear of the LORD is the beginning of wisdom;
   prudent are all who live by it.
   Your praise endures forever.

1 Cor. 2: 9-10

But as it is written:
   "What eye has not seen, and ear has not heard,
      and what has not entered the human heart,
   what God has prepared for those who love him,"
this God has revealed to us through the Spirit.

I praise you Lord! LORD, I place my faith, hope, and trust in you! My God, bless all babies from the moment of conception. We pray to you, Dear Jesus, that these babies are carried to full term and born into this world to live their lives to their fullest, loving and serving you. My Dear Heavenly Mother Mary, you said "Yes" To God's Archangel Gabriel that you would conceive a child in your womb, and, give birth to your son, who would be named Jesus. My Dear God, please bless, and give your love and protection to all mothers and fathers.

My Dear Lord, help mothers who have been victims of rape or incest. I pray, Lord, that if they conceived a child out of rape or incest, not to abort the child, to not use the RU-486 morning after pill, or have any abortifacient drugs given to her at the hospital or at home. I pray, Lord, the mother carries the child in her womb. Dear Lord, I pray they seek immediate help from the authorities and immediate medical attention from a gynecologist or regular doctor for a possible venereal disease (or Aids) they may have received from the rapist or the person involved in incest. Dear Lord, in the majority of the cases in which this happens to a young woman in youth, or an adult woman, they will not be able to afford to raise the child them self (if they are married, the husband may or may not agree to keeping the child to raise). If the mother decides not to keep this precious baby, I pray, Lord, that they place this child up for adoption. We also pray, Dear God, that these mothers who were raped, turn to you in prayer for your counseling, love, and caring for their physical and mental well being; this was an atrocious act committed upon them by the rapist, or through incest. God, I pray, they know they should also seek counseling of a psychologist for their own personal healing.

Dear Jesus, you are our "Jesus of Divine Mercy," and I place my trust in you. Jesus, Our Savior and Redeemer, bless, protect and save the conceived unborn child. Dearest Jesus, you said, **"Do to others whatever you would have them do to you." Matthew 7: 12.** Dearest Jesus, we pray abortionists, their assistants, nurses that assist in abortion procedures, pro-choice advocates, and pro-choice political decision lawmakers in many parts of the world, realize the **seriousness of this HOLY underlined statement you made above in this paragraph.** Dear Lord, may they contemplate their own mother having aborted them. May they realize, Lord, that this fetus is **squirming** and **suffering** for their lives, in first, second and third trimester abortions; they are taken out piece by piece of their bodies, saline abortions, etc., and wondering what's happening to them in **their pain**. I pray, Dear Lord, that the body parts from these aborted babies not be used in any way. I know, Dearest Blessed Trinity, you are very offended by abortions, and, when aborted babies are thrown in garbage cans, garbage bags, or flushed down the toilet; or, abortions done on abortion ships, and these babies are thrown in the waters of the sea.

My Jesus, help the young youth and young adults, especially those in middle schools, junior high schools, high schools, and colleges, to stop and think before they act irrationally. May they know Lord, the use of illegal drugs or homemade concoctions of drugs, cigarette smoking, and alcohol is not good for them to use and, especially if the mother is pregnant; and, this could develop into an addiction I pray, Lord, that youth do not bully a pregnant youth, as this may cause the young woman to have an abortion, to take abortifacient drugs, or commit suicide (killing herself and the baby or babies growing in her womb.) I pray, Holy Spirit, that you illuminate the minds and hearts of our youth and young adults to spend their money wisely; and, do charitable work, piano/musical instrument lessons, voice lessons, theater, reading good books from their school or local library, and healthy sports activities. We pray, Lord, they do not view pornography on the Internet, too much television viewing, indecent movie attendance, or movie rentals that often display a lot of sex. Dear Jesus, I pray that parent's monitor their children's activities, and that children "Honor their Father and their Mother."

I pray, Dearest Jesus, that the youth and young adults in this world seek spirituality in a prayer life, either by praying their Holy Bibles or other Holy Books of prayer, or contemplative prayer. I pray, Dear Jesus, they do not submit to the pressure of their peers; and, not doing things that are not good, healthy and pure for their bodies. Dearest Jesus, it is said in Romans, Chapter 12 of the Holy Bible: **"Do not conform yourself to this age but be transformed by the renewal of your mind, that you may discern** what is the will of God, what is good and pleasing and perfect… Let love be sincere; hate what is evil, hold on to what is good." Rom. Chapter 12: 2, 9

Dearest Holy Mother Mary, I pray that you help and guide mothers-to-be to not be afraid of their pregnancy, but submit to it and say "Yes". I pray to you Blessed Virgin Mary, to help mothers to take good care of their bodies during their pregnancy, as you took good care of your body when you carried your precious son Jesus in your womb. I pray, Dear Mother Mary, for you to intercede to God in prayer to watch over a mother who gives birth to her child in the streets, at home or anywhere other than a hospital; and, that emergency care is there for them. I pray, Holy Spirit, help us to trust in Jesus, move our hearts to loving and caring for others, especially the **poor**; and, to always forgive one another. Amen.

Blessed Virgin Mary, Mother of all nations, pray for us.

Psalm 118: 1, 4, 5, 13-14

Ps, 118: 1, 4, 5, 13-14
Give thanks to the LORD, who is good,
    whose love endures forever.

Let those who fear the LORD say,
    God's love endures forever.

In danger, I called on the LORD;
    the LORD answered me and set me free.

I was hard pressed and falling,
    but the LORD came to my help.
The LORD, my strength and might,
    came to me as savior.

Mt., 6: 34; Ch. 7: 1-2; 7-8; Ch. 14: 14
Do not worry about tomorrow; tomorrow will take care of itself.

Stop judging, that you may not be judged. For as you judge, so will you be judged, and the measure with which you measure will be measured out to you.

"Ask, and it will be given to you; seek and you will find; knock and the door will be opened to you. For everyone who asks, receives; and the one who seeks, finds;

and to the one who knocks, the door will be opened.

When he disembarked and saw the vast crowd, his heart was moved with pity for them, and he cured their sick.

2 Cor, I: 3-7
Blessed be the God and Father of our Lord Jesus Christ, the Father of compassion and God of all encouragement, who encourages us in our every affliction, so that we may be able to encourage those who are in any affliction with the encouragement with which we ourselves are encouraged by God. For as Christ's sufferings overflow to us, so through Christ does our encouragement also overflow. If we are afflicted, it is for your encouragement and salvation; if we are encouraged, it is for your encouragement, which enables you to endure the same sufferings that we suffer. Our hope for you is firm, for we know that as you share in the sufferings, you also share in the encouragement.

CHAPTER SEVEN (7)
DAY SEVEN (7) OF PRAYER

Psalm 115: 1-3
Not to us, LORD, not to us
    but to your name give glory
    because of your faithfulness and love.
Why should the nations say,
    "Where is their God?"
Our God is in heaven;
    whatever God wills is done.

John 12: 1-3
Six days before Passover Jesus came to Bethany, where Lazarus was, whom Jesus had raised from the dead. They gave a dinner for him there, and Martha served, while Lazarus was one of those reclining at table with him. Mary took a liter of costly perfumed oil made from genuine aromatic nard and anointed the feet of Jesus and dried them with her hair; the house was filled with the fragrance of the oil.

James 1: 2-4, 12
Consider it all joy, my brothers, when you encounter various trials, for you know that the testing of your faith produces perseverance. And let perseverance be perfect, so that you may be perfect and complete, lacking in nothing.
Blessed is the man who perseveres in temptation, for when he has been proved

he will receive the crown of life that he promised to those who love him.

My Dear God, bless all mothers who have conceived children, and I pray Mother's give birth to their infants, so that they may have the "right to life." God bless grandparents, or other extended family members who help the mother care for her child. Dear God, bless foster parents or family members who care for children, and caregivers of children who live in orphanages; and, that these children be given much loving care, and no physical, verbal or sexual abuse in these places. Dear Jesus, give adoptive parents many graces and blessings for them and their children, and none of these aforementioned abuses happen to their children. Dear Jesus, all creation is in God's image and likeness and have a God given purpose; and, if they are born handicapped in any way, I pray the Mother and Father keep, love, and care for the child.

I pray, Dear Jesus, that the youth and young adults of the world, if they find out they conceived a child, she is pregnant, for her or him, to never consider suicide (maybe because of fear of parents or grandparents response to her being pregnant). I pray, dear Jesus, that they realize committing suicide would also be the loss of their lives very sadly, as well as the loss of the child growing in the mother's womb. I pray, Dear Lord, that they may not be afraid, knowing they can turn to you and to your precious Mother, the Blessed Virgin Mary, in prayer to help them every step of the way. We pray, Dear Lord, they seek the help of a pro-life center, in keeping the baby growing in the mother's womb, and giving birth to this child. We pray, Jesus, if they can't raise a child at that time of their lives, they know they can place this child up for adoption.

My Dear Jesus Christ, present among us, as you told us, **"I am the light of the world. Whoever follows me will not walk in darkness, but will have the light of life." Jn, 8: 12.** Dear Jesus, I pray, please illumine, guide, protect and keep healthy all pregnant mothers; give them the faith, hope, and trust in you to accept their growing babies in their womb, and give birth to them. Dear Jesus, I pray you instill in the minds and hearts of the Mother and Father of this child, to never consider an abortion procedure, the use of the RU-486 morning after pill, or other abortifacient drugs. **I pray, Dear God, ladies read the warning labels that come with contraceptives; and know these drugs can cause various forms of cancer and other physical problems. I pray, Dear God, ladies also read the warnings that can happen from the use of abortifacient drugs, such as the RU-486 pill that can cause heavy bleeding and other painful complications.** I pray, Dear God, that the Father does not coerce or threaten the mother in any way to take these types of drugs, or have an abortion; or, that the Mother does not take it upon herself to take the RU486 pill, other abortifacient drugs, or have an abortion.

Dear Lord, I pray that you bless single mothers who choose to keep their newborn infant child and give their baby proper care and a loving home. Dear Jesus, I pray for an end to marriages ending up in divorce. I pray, God, for good moral values, an end to swinger's groups, (that even include single people) as this is committing adultery and is immoral; and, this too can contribute to an abortion procedure, use of the RU-486 morning after pill, other abortifacient drugs, or divorce. Dear Mother Mary, we pray, that couples relish the love and commitment they made to each other on their wedding day, to realize the sanctity and holiness of the marriage vows, in sickness and in health, until death do us part. **Dear Jesus, your apostle Paul said: "Love is patient, love is kind. It is not jealous, [love] is not pompous, it is not inflated, it is not rude, it does not seek its own interests, it is not quick-tempered, it does not brood over injury, it does not rejoice over wrongdoing but rejoices with the truth. It bears all things, believes all things, hopes all things, endures all things… So faith, hope, love remain, these three; but the greatest of these is love." <u>1 Cor. 13: 4-7, 13</u>** Dear Jesus, I pray couples when having difficulties in their relationship, that they **<u>not</u>** seek an immediate separation or divorce, but seek your help first in prayer and seek marital counseling. I pray, Dear Jesus, that if either one has addictions to such things as a compulsive drug use problem, outside of marriage sexual addiction, alcohol, or gambling, they seek help in rehabilitation services and other treatment programs. I pray, LORD, they understand that this life style addiction problem will tell them "we can't afford to have this child now;" and, they will pursue an abortion, using abortifacient drugs; and, this will affect their emotional well being in that this child is not a part of their life to care for and love. Dear LORD, you gave us as part of your ten commandments: **"You shall not kill" "You shall not commit adultery," <u>Exodus, Ch. 20: 13, 14.</u>**

I pray, Dear Lord, parents teach their children about prayer, their morning and evening prayers, before meal prayers and **to have family prayer time every day, the Holy Bible**, and/or other holy books of prayer; and, have more open communications as a married couple, and quality time with their children. I pray, Dear Jesus that Catholic families and other Christian religions that pray the prayers of the Holy Rosary, to pray daily these prayers the Blessed Virgin Mary gave us; these are wonderful family prayers too, besides individual or group prayers. God listens and acts on these and other prayers given by his Blessed Mother Mary in her many intercessory prayer petitions to God for help to us, and for the conversion of sinners back to God.

I pray, Lord, you bless divorced parents and guide them, through the Holy Spirit, as this is hard for both of the parents and their children. I pray for the children in the family, that these children need to spend time with both parents. I pray, Lord, that in an divorced situation, or in marriage abusive situation, where there is verbal, physical, or sexual abuse by one or both of the parents to their children;

or, a relative to the children, that a safe environment is provided for the child/ children. I pray, Dear LORD, if parents are going through a divorce and find out a teenage daughter of theirs is pregnant during this time, that they advise her **NOT** to have an abortion. I pray that they provide for her in a loving and caring manner, and have her baby placed up for adoption. Dear God I pray that mothers do not abandon their newborns in a garbage can or any other way of disposing the child

<u>Dear Jesus, you said:</u> "Amen, I say to you, unless you turn and become like children, you will not enter the kingdom of heaven. Whoever humbles himself like this child is the greatest in the kingdom of heaven. And whoever receives one child such as this in my name receives me." <u>Matt 18: 3-5</u>

Dear Lord, I pray that you also help women (often youth to young adults) who have eating disorder problems, such as bulimia, anorexia, binge eating, or compulsive overeating, to instill in their hearts that they need medical assistance and counseling to overcome these disorders. I pray, Dear Lord, young women and adult women realize that in the event the mother is pregnant and has any of the above disorders, this may lead her to taking the RU-486 pill, abortifacient drugs, an abortion; or, the danger of a miscarriage, or stillborn baby as she is not taking proper care of her health.

I pray, Dear Lord, married couples acknowledge that love, communication and setting a good example for their children are important. I pray, Lord, for them, to **NOT** consider an abortion if they were surprised by having another pregnancy, or learned in any way early on in the pregnancy that the child would be handicapped, or that they didn't have the financial means to care for another child. I pray, Dear LORD, parents never say to one of their children, "we didn't want you, you were an accident and we should have aborted you," as this would have long devastating hurt in their heart and mind.

I pray, Blessed Virgin Mary, that you show them that Jesus said: **"I am the way and the truth and the life," <u>Jn 14: 6</u>** and advise them to **"Do whatever he tells you." <u>Jn 2: 5</u>**. I know, Dear Jesus, you love me very much; and, may every day I return my love to you.

I pray, Holy Spirit, that morally correct thoughts of prolife be given to people who perform abortions, assist in abortions, nurses who assist in abortion procedures; and, teenage girls and women who want to pursue an abortion, pro-choice advocates in government making decision powers, and pro-choice advocates.

Blessed Virgin Mary, Mother of all nations, pray for us.

I Cor. 10: 7-9
And do not become idolaters, as some of them did, as it is written, "The people sat down to eat and drink, and rose up to revel." Let us not indulge in immorality as some of them did, and twenty-three thousand fell within a single day. Let us not test Christ as some of them did, and suffered death by serpents.

Proverbs 5: 18, 20-23
And have joy of the wife of your youth,
Why then, my son, should you go astray for another's wife
     and accept the embraces of an adulteress?

For each man's ways are plain to the LORD'S sight;
     all their paths he surveys;
By his own inequities the wicked man will be caught,
     in the meshes of his own sin he will be held fast;
He will die from lack of discipline,
     through the greatness of his folly he will be lost.

Psalm 40: 2-4, 6, 12-14
I waited, waited for the LORD;
    who bent down and heard my cry,
Drew me out of the pit of destruction,
    out of the mud of the swamp,
Set my feet upon rock,
    steadied my steps,
And put a new song in my mouth,
    a hymn to our God.
Many shall look on in awe
    and they shall trust in the LORD.

How numerous, O LORD, my God,
    you have made your wondrous deeds!
And in your plans for us,
    there is none to equal you.
Should I wish to declare or tell them,
    too many are they to recount.

LORD, do not withhold your compassion from me;
    may your enduring kindness ever preserve me.

For all about me are evils beyond count;
   my sins so overcome me I cannot see.
They are more than the hairs of my head;
   my courage fails me.

LORD, graciously rescue me!
   Come quickly to help me, LORD!

CHAPTER EIGHT (8)
DAY EIGHT OF PRAYER

Psalm 16: 1-2, 7-11

Keep me safe, O God;
   in you I take refuge.
I say to the LORD,
   you are my Lord,
   you are my only good.

I bless the LORD who counsels me…
I keep the LORD always before me;
   with the LORD at my right, I shall never be shaken.
Therefore, my heart is glad, my soul rejoices;
   my body also dwells secure,
For you will not abandon me to Sheol,
   nor let your faithful servant see the pit.
You will show me the path to life,
   abounding joy in your presence,
   the delights at your right hand forever.

Ps 19: 8-12
The law of the LORD is perfect,
   refreshing the soul.
The decree of the LORD is trustworthy,
   giving wisdom to the simple.
The precepts of the LORD are right,
   rejoicing the heart.
The command of the LORD is clear,
   enlightening the eye.

The fear of the LORD is pure,
    enduring forever.
The statutes of the LORD are true,
    all of them just;
More desirable than gold,
    than a hoard of purest gold,

Sweeter also than honey
    or drippings from the comb.

By them your servant is instructed;
    obeying them brings much reward.

I praise, worship and adore you LORD! I place my faith, hope and trust in you. My Dear God, bless mothers everywhere; also, the ones who have aborted their babies, and, that they express sorrow for this sin. I pray, Lord, you give them strength and love through this hurt in their hearts for aborting their child. Dear Jesus, through your Blessed Mother Mary interceding to you for us, protect women who have conceived a child from any man or woman demanding that they abort the child, use the RU-486 morning after pill, or other abortifacient drugs. Dearest Jesus, we know the aforementioned statement can also be of the reverse, where the father of the child wants the child, and the mother wants the abortion. I pray, Dear God that we realize that we all have the Blessed Virgin Mary as Our heavenly Mother watching out for her children here on this earth.

Dear LORD, we all have trials and temptations in our lives; Jesus, you know we are weak and sin, please help me to always repent of my sins, and to seek your merciful forgiveness. Help us, Lord, to turn to you in prayer for our needs. Dear Lord, I pray you turn our hearts to the Holy Spirit to guide us and enlighten our weariness and bring our lives to **hope in prayer.** My Dear Jesus, I turn my eyes to your beautiful and wonderful face; I place my faith, hope and trust in you.

Dear God, I pray that soon the 1973 United States Supreme Court decision of ROE VS. WADE be REVERSED, making it ILLEGAL for mothers to abort their conceived child; and, for decisions made by OTHER GOVENMENTS where abortions are legal in the WORLD, to make ANY ABORTION PROCEDURE ILLEGAL, if it is LEGAL. I pray, Dear God, that "Life beginning at Conception" type of laws respecting the sanctity and holiness of every life conceived in the mother's womb be passed all over the world in countries approving abortion. I pray, Dear Lord that this law is passed making any type of abortion procedure illegal (unless the mother's life is in danger). I pray, Dear Lord, more adoption centers be set up for a loving and caring family to adopt a child. I pray, Dear Jesus, that people's taxpayer funds, and health insurance plans are not used to fund any types of abortions, the RU-486 morning after pill, or other abortifacient drugs.

Dear LORD, I pray that boyfriends or spouses are spiritually healed when they found out that a pregnant woman in their lives had an abortion. I pray, Dear Lord, both sides of the man or woman's family, the grandparents, siblings, aunts, uncles, and friends, are all consoled and healed, to include them forgiving the mother who had the abortion. I pray, Dear Lord, people realize that the mother, in making this decision to have this abortion procedure done, suffers from this emotional loss in her life. I pray, Dear Jesus, that we can be your disciples and administer our own love, healing and forgiveness to those that are hurting in any way in their lives.

I pray, Dear Jesus, when abortionists perform an abortion, and the baby is born alive, that they don't proceed to kill the baby; examples: cutting their heads off, cutting their spinal cords, or other means of killing this baby that came out alive. I pray, Dear Jesus, they understand, that by making sure this "born alive baby" will be killed, that "The Blessed Trinity" is severely hurt by all of these actions. I pray, Dearest Jesus, Christians understand, through your Passion and Death on the Cross, you have died for our sins, so that we might be saved. I pray, Lord, that they express sorrow and repent of these sins, never to have these beliefs and do the killing of the baby born alive procedures again. **"For as often as you eat this bread and drink the cup, you proclaim the death of the Lord until he comes. Therefore whoever eats the bread or drinks the cup of the Lord unworthily will have to answer for the body and blood of the Lord. A person should examine himself, and so eat the bread and drink the cup. For anyone who eats and drinks without discerning the body, eats and drinks judgment on himself. <u>1 Cor. 11: 26-29.</u>**

I thank you God for the precious gift of life. I place my pro-life prayers to you on your alter in heaven, God, through the intercessory prayer help of Jesus Sacred Heart, and, Mother Mary's Immaculate Heart. I pray, **<u>St. Joseph</u>**, Mother Mary's most chaste spouse and foster father of Jesus, and, **<u>patron saint of the dying</u>**, for an **<u>end</u>** to abortion. I pray, Dear Lord, that the RU-486 morning after pill, abortifacient drugs, euthanasia, embryonic stem cell research, cloning of any kind; and, using aborted baby's body parts to other humans or any type of medical research, be ended. I pray, Dear Lord, people know and understand one of your commandments is: **"You shall not kill." <u>Exodus Ch. 20: 13</u>**, always be recognized; and that killing of a conceived child in the mother's womb is **<u>"murder,"</u>** a mortal (severe) sin.

I pray, Jesus, people realize that any one who coerces or threatens a mother to having an abortion, or a mother seeking and having an abortion, that this is murder to the child; **and, pro-choice advocates change their ideas, thoughts and actions, that abortion is a "woman's choice or right." I pray, Dear Lord that women understand that this is NOT a "woman's choice or right", as this child was conceived in God's image and likeness, and is meant to be born into this world. I pray, Dear LORD, people realize, that you decide the moment each person is to be called home for everlasting peace, joy and love.**

I pray, Blessed Virgin Mary, that love, compassion, understanding, and Our Lord's mercy be given to mothers who have experienced an abortion procedure or the use of abortifacient drugs, such as the 486 morning after pill. I pray, Lord, that abortionists, their assistants and nurses who assist in abortion procedures, change their jobs in their life to that of a healthy and holy mission. I know, Merciful Lord, you have mercy and forgiveness for these people when they repent of these sins; and, with a firm intent not to believe in or perform abortions again. **I pray, Dearest Jesus, we all know we are held accountable to God, on our day of judgment when we meet God face to face; and, that we your people on earth are _never_ to _judge_ one another.**

Dear God, I know that **Satan (the Devil) and his evil spirits** wish to keep places of abortion open in areas of the world, where these malicious acts of murder are occurring on God's precious conceived babies in the mother's womb. **Dear Lord,** I pray that **Satan** no longer will convince these doctors, their assistants, and nurses who assist in abortion procedures, to murder babies in the mother's womb.

I pray, **Dear Lord** that abortionists, their assistants, nurses who assist in abortion procedures, and all pro-choice activists will be against **Satan** by turning their hearts, minds, and souls back to you **LORD**. I pray, Dear God, these evil hurting and painful acts to the conceived child be ended; and, I ask this through Jesus Christ, the intercession of the Blessed Virgin Mary, and St. Joseph. Dear St. Michael, The Archangel, I pray for your protection to us from the evils of **Satan**, and all of his prowling spirits seeking the ruin of souls. I pray, blessed Virgin Mary, you enlighten our minds that Jesus said: **"I am the way and the truth and the life," Jn 14:6** and advise us to **"Do whatever he tells you." Jn 2:5. Amen. My Jesus, I worship, praise, adore and love you!**
I pray, Holy Spirit, for you to illuminate and renew your seven gifts to us.

St. Gerard Majella, Patron Saint of Expectant Mothers, pray for us.
St. Joseph, Patron Saint of numerous causes, to include the Dying,
Pray for us.
Blessed Virgin Mary, Our Lady of Perpetual Help, pray for us, and for the

protection of the unborn conceived child.
Blessed Virgin Mary, Queen of The Holy Rosary, pray for us. Blessed Virgin
Mary, our Lady of Fatima, pray for us.
Blessed Virgin Mary, Mother of all nations, pray for us.

Isaiah 55: 6-9
Seek the LORD while he may be found,
    call him while he is near.
Let the scoundrel forsake his way,
    and the wicked man his thoughts;
Let him turn to the LORD for mercy;
    to our God who is generous in forgiving.
For my thoughts are not your thoughts,
    nor are your ways my ways, says the LORD.
As high as the heavens are above the earth,
    so high are my ways above your ways
    and my thoughts above your thoughts.

Psalm 145: 1-2, 7-10, 17-18
Praise. Of David.
I will extol you, my God and king;
    I will bless your name forever.
Every day I will bless you;
    I will praise your name forever.
They publish the renown of your abounding goodness
    and joyfully sing of your justice.
The LORD is gracious and merciful,
    slow to anger and abounding in love.
The LORD is good to all,
    compassionate to every creature.
All your works give you thanks, O LORD,
    and your faithful bless you.
You, LORD, are just in all your ways,
    faithful in all your works.

You, LORD, are near to all who call upon you,
      to all who call upon you in truth.

Phil 2: 1-11
If there is any encouragement in Christ, any solace in love, any participation in
the Spirit, any compassion and mercy, complete my joy by being of the same

mind, with the same love, united in heart, thinking one thing. Do nothing out of selfishness or out of vainglory; rather, humbly regard others as more important than yourselves, each looking out not for his own interests, but [also] everyone for those of others.

Have among yourselves the same attitude that is also yours in Christ Jesus,
Who, though he was in the form of God,
    did not regard equality with God
       something to be grasped.
    Rather, he emptied himself,
       taking the form of a slave,
       coming in human likeness;
       and found human in appearance,
       he humbled himself,
       becoming obedient to death,
          even death on a cross.
Because of this, God greatly exalted
       him
       and bestowed on him the name
       that is above every name,
    that at the name of Jesus
       every knee should bend,
       of those in heaven and on earth and
          under the earth,
    and every tongue confess that
       Jesus Christ is Lord,
       to the glory of God the Father.

CHAPTER NINE (9)
DAY NINE (9) OF PRAYER

NOTE: These prayers of <u>Chapter (day) nine (9)</u> can be prayed nine consecutive days by <u>non-Christians</u> and give these prayers directly to God.

Those <u>Christians</u> who don't believe in intercessory prayers to God by the Blessed Virgin Mary and the Saints for our needs, they do not have to use their intercessory help; but, they can substitute the Virgin Mary's and other saints--the first eight days of prayers directly to God, Jesus, the Holy Spirit, or the Blessed Trinity. And, they also should then pray Chapter 9 (the ninth day of prayer).

<u>Christians</u> who do believe in the intercessory help for their prayer petitions to the Blessed Virgin Mary and the Saints to God, Jesus or the Holy Spirit, can say all nines days of prayer as written.

I praise and worship you God, Our Lord of All Nations! To you, my Lord GOD, I give all glory and honor, now, and forever! LORD, I put my hope in you! Dear God, thank you for the precious gift of sanctity and holiness in every life!

Dear God, bless all mothers who have conceived a child and have them nourish their bodies appropriately during their pregnancy. If these mothers, Dear God, can't care for their new born infants, or their parents help if able, have them place the child up for **adoption, foster care or an orphanage.**

I pray, God that neither of the parent's abandons the child at birth. I pray, God, that the parents never consider abortion, the use of the RU-486 morning after pill, or abortifacient drugs. I pray, Dear God, the youth and adults never consider the option of committing suicide of their own bodies after learning the mother is pregnant; and, she is afraid, or afraid of what her parents would say, as this would lead to the loss of precious lives. I pray, that they turn to God in prayer, first as their Father in heaven; and, be made known that there are therapists, and pro-life centers available for them.

I pray, Dear God, that you have all women (and in their young youth) know that all life conceived in the mother's womb is precious to you, and this life was created in your image and likeness. I pray, Dear LORD, you have them become aware that it is a mortal (serious) sin to abort their child, thus killing the child growing in their womb from the moment of conception; and, of how many emotional effects they will suffer. I pray, Dear God, women and teenage girls understand that harm may have been done to their female reproductive organs; also, infections, bleeding, because of unsanitary conditions where the abortion is performed, and possible death of the mother. Dear Lord, I pray the mother's aren't brainwashed or coerced into having this abortion procedure, taking the RU-486 morning after pill, or abortifacient drugs.

I pray, Dear Lord, that all countries in the world that legalize abortion, pass new laws to make abortions of any kind, even the RU-486 morning after pill or abortifacient drugs **<u>illegal</u>**. Dear God, we pray that the **<u>"Roe vs. Wade"</u>** law passed by the U.S. Supreme Court be **<u>reversed</u>**; and, that **<u>"Respect Life from Conception"</u>** laws be passed; and these laws are never allowed being reversed. Dear God, I pray that everyone has a **<u>"Right to Life,"</u>** as we are all created in your image and likeness.

I pray, Dear LORD, you have pregnant mothers realize, that if their own mother had aborted them, they wouldn't be here to abort their child, or to live their lives to the fullest, loving and serving you God. I pray, Dear God, that people who are pro-choice advocates never advise a mother to have an abortion of any kind, including the taking of the RU-486 pill, or abortifacient drugs. I pray, Dear LORD, pro-choice clinics or hospitals, **DO NOT PERFORM ABORTIONS, OR, GIVE A LIST OF ABORTIONISTS IN THE AREA.** I pray, Dear God, for all mothers who have had an abortion; God, you are loving, caring and merciful, and I pray you give your great love and care to them at this difficult time in their lives. I pray, Dear God, for people to pray for teenage girls and women who have had an abortion, the RU486 morning after pill or other abortifacient drugs, (when they are in fear that they may be pregnant); this loss in their lives will be emotionally hurting, and they may have been physically hurt from the abortion procedure. I pray, Dear LORD, the mother who has conceived a child, uses her own good common sense, not be afraid, and seeks the help and guidance of people working at a pro-life center. May they realize God; you are their Father in heaven, and ready at every moment to help them. I pray, God, that contraceptives, and the RU-486 morning after pill, **<u>NOT be given out or provided access to</u>** our young girls, and young adult women, in middle schools, high schools or colleges. I pray, Lord, that medical insurance and drug plans will not provide insurance payment to companies or small business employers for any RU-486 morning after drugs or any abortifacient drugs.

I pray, Dear LORD, that you help mothers to love the baby growing in their womb, feeling it's kicking and moving around as it grows, and to anxiously await the birth of this child; and, not deciding to abort the child. I pray, Dear LORD, if a mother does abort her child, she expresses sorrow and repents of this sin of abortion. I pray, Dear God, for your compassion and love to her, as she sometimes does not think clearly, she may be threatened to have an abortion, and she's under much stress and anxiety over this decision she has to make. I pray, God, she gives her aborted child a name, and know she can pray to this child asking for help in issues in her life, so this child can take her petitions to God.in prayer. I pray, God, for your special mercy, and kind love to her if she dies from the abortion procedure. I pray, Dear Lord, that in often regretting the decision of having an abortion, she and the father seek emotional healing in prayers to you, Lord, and individual or group therapy.

I pray, God, for parents of youth in many parts of the world, because they need money to support the family, do **<u>not</u>** send their daughters (often very young) to become prostitutes; and, they realize, their daughter may get pregnant and have an abortion, or she may seek abortifacient drugs.

I pray, Dear Lord, that there isn't the loss of the lives or severe infections of mothers who go through the abortion procedure, as some abortion clinics are unclean and unsanitary; and, the doctors may not even be medically licensed doctors, or there may just be nurses doing the abortion procedure. I pray, LORD, that abortionists, their assistants and nurses be made aware of the fact, that they may not only be killing the conceived infant in the mother's womb, but may be injuring the mother, and/or causing her to lose her life.

I pray, Dear God, you instill in the hearts of these abortionists, assistants, and nurses that assist in abortion procedures, that these are grievous **mortal sins** which are very bad for their souls; and, that they need to quit this job, repent for all these sins of abortion, and seek your merciful forgiveness. We pray, **Dear** God, if they have office secretaries and accountants, that these workers quit these jobs. I pray, Lord, that all these people amend their lives to doing a mission that is holy and serving, loving and respectful of the mother's life, and the new life of the conceived child in the mother's womb. I pray, Dear LORD, for them too, to seek emotional help from you in prayer, counseling and direction for hope in their lives when they repent and seek your merciful forgiveness. **I pray, Dear Lord, they never resume or recommend an abortion to a mother again; and, please guide them to a new job, helping mothers to give birth to babies again, or to jobs that are morally right in seeking their new careers.** I pray, Dear God, that they realize that you too love them, and want them to change their ways to be holy and prayerful people to you God. I pray, Dear GOD, that you have them become aware that they too, do not know the day, the hour or the moment they will be called home to you for their judgment day; none of us sinners know, as we are all sinners, in the way we are sinning that is serious and very offensive to you. Dear God, I pray, you help them become aware that any of us could die suddenly of a massive heart attack, a massive stroke, an aneurysm, a bad car or airplane crash, biking or walking across the street and getting hit by a car, etc.

I pray, Dear Lord GOD, that **administrators providing** for the pro-choice people working in pro-choice places or clinics, doctors who perform abortions in these clinics or hospitals (that provide these services for abortionists, assistants and nurses who assist in the abortion procedures to use), **to not believe in or promote the use of their facilities to destroy the little innocents in the mother's womb's.** I pray, Dear LORD that administrators awaken their hearts and minds to know this thinking of murdering or approving of murdering the precious little ones, who are trying to grow in their mother's wombs is **MURDER**, a violation of one of your commandments, "You shall not kill." **Exodus 20: 13.** I pray, Dear God, they realize this also brings **much hurt to you, in that you created us in your image and likeness to live, love, and serve you.** I pray, Dear **LORD**, that they realize that **SATAN**, the **DEVIL**, and his **evil spirits** roaming about the world, always produces evil or entice evil into our lives, by telling us that greed, materialism, our own power and control, is more important than a precious gift of a baby's life brought into this world. Dear **LORD GOD,** instill in their minds and hearts that **SATAN** is out to destroy as many souls as he can in this world for himself. I pray, God, that people realize that Satan wants these evil acts done; or, believing, assisting, or promoting these evil acts of **ABORTION** as **"being alright to do."** "I know, Dear God, <u>they are NO ONE'S right, or the Mother's right</u>," as <u>Satan, the Devil, and his evil spirits</u> tells her: **you have a woman's choice, it's your body, and you can do what you want with it.** Dear God, we pray, many people stop using the word that's become very **"liberal in their way of thinking," "CHOICE"**; or they say, **"IT'S MY CHOICE", (and both times can be related to proper thinking or irrational thinking in many of our decisions), but BOTH RELATED VERY MANY TIMES TO PRO-CHOICE for abortions.** Dearest God, I pray, that people understand that the word "**CHOICE**" may violate **YOUR TEN (10) COMMANDMENTS YOU GAVE US THROUGH MOSES TO FOLLOW, AND KEEP THESE COMMANDMENTS. Exodus 20: 1-17. Dear Lord, I pray, that teenagers and adult women realize that destroying a conceived child in their womb by the use of abortion, the RU-486 morning after pill, abortifacient drugs, or any way to abort the child, is very evil and wrong. Dear Lord, I pray that there be NO selling of aborted baby parts, encouraging or promoting embryonic stem cell research, euthanasia, cloning, or anything harmful to one's life to never be done.** We pray, Dear God, they convert to <u>**pro-life, that they are sorry, seek your merciful forgiveness for these sins, and want to amend their life to do what is holy and pleasing to you, GOD, as they too are your children. I pray, Dear LORD that you tell them: "I desire you to be holy, loving, and caring, and not killing (or believing in killing) the little innocent ones conceived life in the mother's wombs."**</u>

I pray, Dearest GOD, that abortionists, their assistants and nurses that assist in abortion procedures, realize abortion procedures for these **little precious ones,** that they have much **pain and suffering,** struggling and squirming about in the womb; they were content sucking their thumbs and moving about freely. I pray, <u>**Dear Lord, that this cold, uncaring, unloving "culture of death" comes to an end; this is an "act of terror" on the innocent ones growing in their mother's wombs.**</u> I pray, Dear LORD that they convert their hearts and souls back to you, and say **"no to the evil one, Satan, the Devil, and his evil spirits prowling about the world, and seeking the destruction of souls.**

Dear LORD, I pray, abortionists, their assistants, nurses that assist in the abortion procedures, politicians responsible for legalizing abortion in countries, where this procedure is legal, and pro-choice advocates, should **love themselves first, and seek affirmative things about themselves that can be instilled in them by you always in their own hearts and souls.** May they, Dearest LORD, prepare a list of positive, healthy and loving things about themselves, go over this list often; and, have them give you these things about themselves, and all they do each day in **love and service to you.** I pray, Dear Lord, they examine past issues in their lives that were hurting to them in their childhood possibly, their teen or young adult years; maybe those years they didn't feel worthwhile, were bullied at school, and felt unloved and unwanted by a parent or both parents. Dear Lord, I pray that we understand that some of them possibly could have been physically, sexually, or verbally abused those years of their life by their parent's or others; or, may have lost a brother or sister when they knew their mother had an abortion. I pray, Dear LORD, that they surrender those sad, unloved and unwanted feelings to you, and that you ask them to seek therapy on these issues; and then, to forgive in their hearts and minds those who were abusive to them. I pray, God, they let go of these sad issues (as difficult as it is to do) and move on in their lives in a positive manner with daily prayers to you, seeking your constant love and direction. I pray, Lord, that people realize how many lives are **lost to abortion each day, as these lives are very important to you, being created in your image and likeness. Dear Lord, I pray that people understand that <u>their little innocent life never had a chance to live here on earth to love and serve you and to have descendants of their own.</u>**

Dear God, please keep us holy, as you are, and that we can sing your praises, worship, adore, serve you and love you, for ever and ever, Amen. **Dear God, I know you have given each human life a free will, but also with this free will, you have given us ten (10) commandments to follow in our lives.** Dear God, I pray we **<u>choose</u>** following your ten (10) commandments and to seek your daily help in prayer. I pray, Dear Lord, that when we meet you face to face, we can be seen by you as your "loving, forgiving, and caring about one another" children on earth.

I pray, Dear LORD, that I remember to express an act of sorrow often, amend my life, and seek your mercy and forgiveness; and, I know GOD, you are ready at every moment in our lives to hear us, to communicate with us, and to bring peace and joy to our hearts and souls. I pray, Dear God, we take at least thirty minutes every day to pray our Holy Bibles or Holy Books of prayer. I pray, God, help us communicate to you our needs, tell you of our happy and sad moments; and, realize, if our needs we ask for in prayer are not obtained, I should accept your holy will for us. I pray, Dear Lord, that I should always place my faith, hope, and trust in you; and, give you thanksgiving in our daily lives. Help us, Dear God, to be holy, humble, and faithful to you. I pray, Dear God, we have a "culture of pro-life."

Dear GOD, I thank you for your love, graces and blessings in our lives; and, my Dear Lord, I love, adore, worship, praise and honor you! Dear God, you are the light of the world! Thank you for your compassion and mercy for us, Dear Lord! Hallelujah! Lord, you are very precious to me! Thank you, Lord God, for your precious gift of life!

Isaiah Chapter 56: 1-7 The Lord's House Open To All
Is 56: 1-7

Thus says the LORD:
Observe what is right, do what is just;
 for my salvation is about to come,
 my justice, about to be revealed.
Happy is the man who does this,
 the son of man who holds to it;
Who keeps the sabbath free from profanation,
 and his hand from any evildoing.
Let not the foreigner say,
 when he would join himself to the LORD,
 "The LORD will surely exclude me from his people";
Nor let the eunuch say,
 "See, I am a dry tree."
 For thus says the LORD:
To the eunuchs who observe my sabbaths
 and choose what pleases me
 and hold fast to my covenant,
I will give, in my house
 and within my walls, a monument and a name
Better than sons and daughters;
 an eternal, imperishable name will I give them.
And the foreigners who join themselves to the LORD,
 ministering to him,
Loving the name of the LORD,
 and becoming his servants---

All who keep the Sabbath free from profanation
      and hold to my covenant,
Them I will bring to my holy mountain
      and make joyful in my house of prayer;
Their holocausts and sacrifices
      will be acceptable on my altar,
For my house shall be called
      a house of prayer for all peoples.

Printed in the United States
By Bookmasters